Colin Churchill was born in Dorchester in 1927 in Monmouth Road and was educated at Miss Kensett's kindergarten school in Great Western Road and from 1937 – 1944 at the Dorchester Grammar School where he was a member of the school OTC/JTC.

He entered Lloyds Bank in 1944, serving as a manager in Devon, Dorset and Somerset before becoming an inspector based in Winchester, covering London and the South of England – a total of forty three and a half years, returning on retirement to his home town.

He married a Dorchester girl, Charlotte Gillingham of Damers Road, by whom he had two sons, Peter and Paul. Sadly she died at a young age. He now lives only a stone's throw from where he was born with his present wife, Pauline.

He is passionate about his home town and takes an active part in helping to fashion its future. This book, which records how he remembers Dorchester in the war years, 1939 – 1945, was written as an attempt to give something back to the town which has given him so much pleasure.

His other books are *British Army Collar Badges 1881 to the present* (1986), and *History of the British Army Infantry Collar Badge* (2001). He has also contributed various articles relating to Military Units connected with Dorset.

Following page
Looking north along Cornhill towards the Town Pump
shortly after the war.

DORCHESTER
VERSUS HITLER

A Country Town goes to War

COLIN CHURCHILL

THE DOVECOTE PRESS

This book is dedicated to my parents Lilian Gertrude and Frederick Churchill for their love and care during the Second World War, to my present wife Pauline who supported me through the research, and writing of this book, and to the residents of Dorchester from 1939-1945 who supported their loved ones who were in the armed forces and away from them – sometimes years at a stretch, who endured the shortages and privations with such cheerfulness and stoicism.

First published in 2006 by The Dovecote Press Ltd
Stanbridge, Wimborne Minster, Dorset BH21 4JD

ISBN 1 904349 44 7

© Colin Churchill 2006

The author has asserted his rights under the Copyright, Designs
and Patent Act 1988 to be identified as author of this work

Designed by The Dovecote Press
Printed and bound in Singapore

All papers used by The Dovecote Press are natural, recyclable products
made from wood grown in sustainable, well-managed forests

A CIP catalogue record for this book is available
from the British Library

1 3 5 7 9 8 6 4 2

Contents

1 The Darkening Storm 12

2 War is Declared 22

3 The Phoney War 36

4 Dunkirk 42

5 Invasion Threatens 44

6 The Battle of Britain 58

7 Local Defense Volunteers, Home Guard, Auxiliary Units 63

8 Air Raids and Bomb Damage 67

9 The War Continues 74

10 But Life Goes On 79

11 The 'Yanks' Arrive 92

12 Preparations for D-Day 97

13 D-Day to Victory 101

14 VE Day 103

15 VJ Day 105

16 The Aftermath 107

Appendix Dorchester as it was in 1939 108

Acknowledgements 122

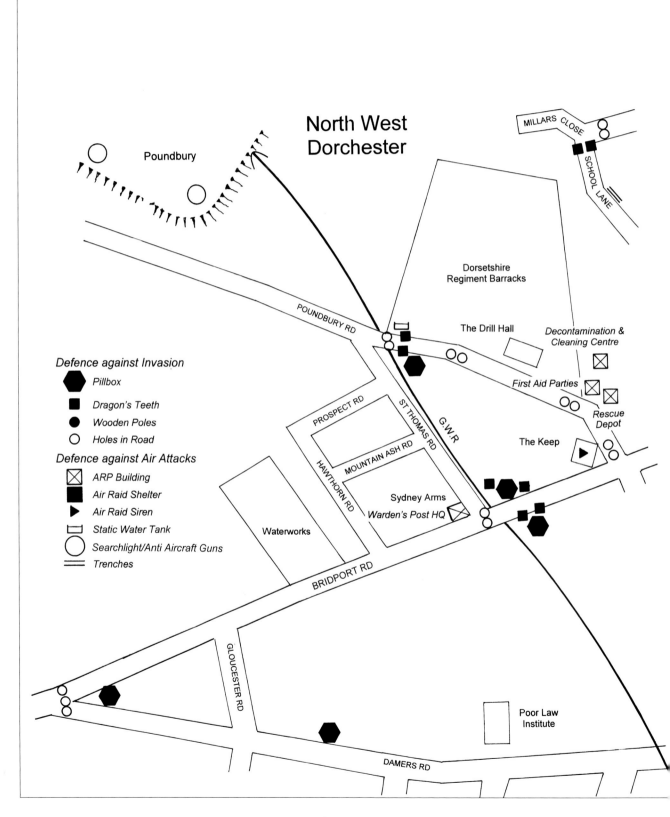

North West Dorchester

Poundbury

MILLARS CLOSE

SCHOOL LANE

Dorsetshire
Regiment Barracks

POUNDBURY RD

The Drill Hall

Decontamination &
Cleaning Centre

Defence against Invasion

⬡ Pillbox

■ Dragon's Teeth

● Wooden Poles

○ Holes in Road

First Aid Parties

Defence against Air Attacks

⊠ ARP Building

■ Air Raid Shelter

▶ Air Raid Siren

⊔ Static Water Tank

○ Searchlight/Anti Aircraft Guns

≡ Trenches

PROSPECT RD

ST THOMAS RD

G.W.R

Rescue
Depot

The Keep

HAWTHORN RD

MOUNTAIN ASH RD

Sydney Arms

Warden's Post HQ

Waterworks

BRIDPORT RD

GLOUCESTER RD

Poor Law
Institute

DAMERS RD

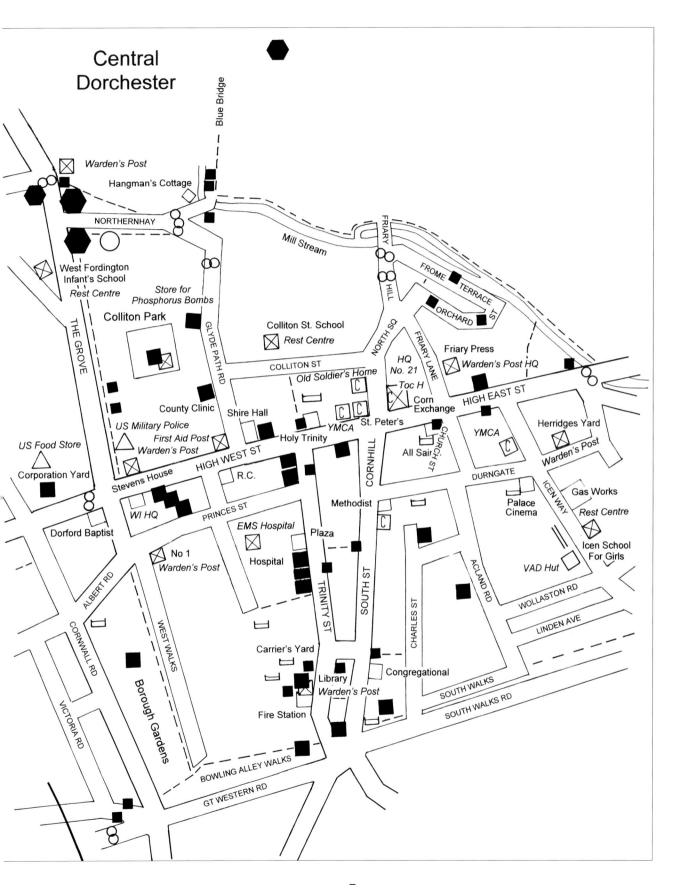

Central Dorchester

Blue Bridge

Warden's Post

Hangman's Cottage

NORTHERNHAY

Mill Stream

West Fordington Infant's School
Rest Centre

Store for Phosphorus Bombs

THE GROVE

Colliton Park

GLYDE PATH RD

Colliton St. School
Rest Centre

COLLITON ST

Old Soldier's Home

FRIARY

HILL

FROME TERRACE

ORCHARD ST

NORTH SQ

FRIARY LANE

Friary Press
Warden's Post HQ

HQ No. 21

Toc H

Corn Exchange

HIGH EAST ST

County Clinic

US Military Police

First Aid Post
Warden's Post

US Food Store

Corporation Yard

Shire Hall

HIGH WEST ST

Holy Trinity

Stevens House

R.C.

YMCA

St. Peter's

CORNHILL

All Saints

CHURCH ST

YMCA

DURNGATE

Herridges Yard

Warden's Post

Gas Works

ICEN WAY

Rest Centre

Palace Cinema

WI HQ

PRINCES ST

Dorford Baptist

ALBERT RD

No 1
Warden's Post

EMS Hospital

Hospital

Plaza

Methodist

SOUTH ST

TRINITY ST

CHARLES ST

ACLAND RD

VAD Hut

Icen School For Girls

WOLLASTON RD

LINDEN AVE

CORNWALL RD

VICTORIA RD

WEST WALKS

Borough Gardens

Carrier's Yard

Library
Warden's Post

Fire Station

Congregational

SOUTH WALKS

SOUTH WALKS RD

BOWLING ALLEY WALKS

GT WESTERN RD

7

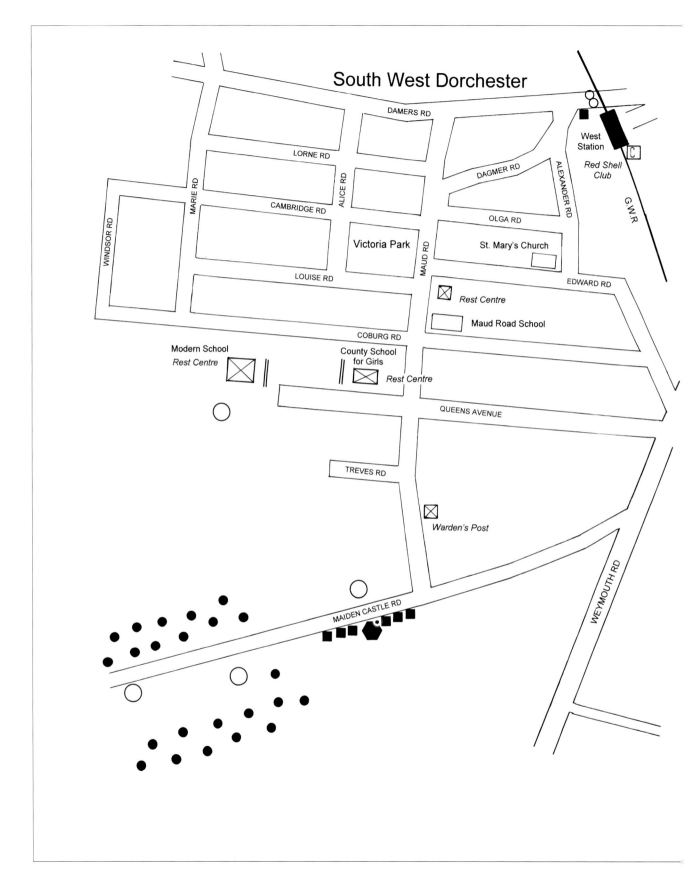

South West Dorchester

DAMERS RD

LORNE RD

MARIE RD

ALICE RD

DAGMER RD

ALEXANDER RD

West Station

Red Shell Club

G.W.R

WINDSOR RD

CAMBRIDGE RD

OLGA RD

Victoria Park

MAUD RD

St. Mary's Church

LOUISE RD

EDWARD RD

Rest Centre

Maud Road School

COBURG RD

Modern School
Rest Centre

County School for Girls
Rest Centre

QUEENS AVENUE

TREVES RD

Warden's Post

MAIDEN CASTLE RD

WEYMOUTH RD

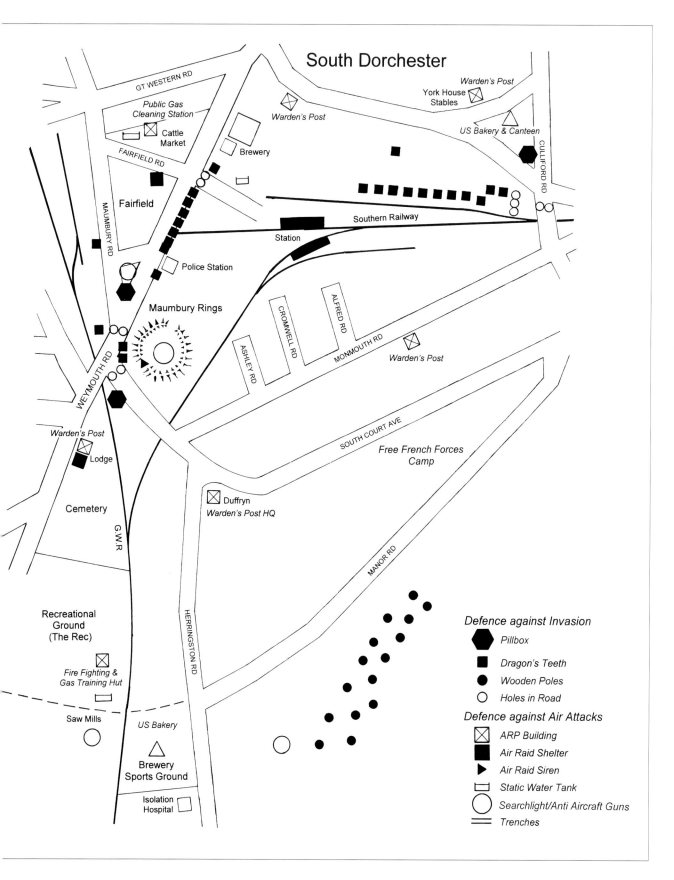

South Dorchester

GT WESTERN RD

Public Gas
Cleaning Station

Cattle
Market

FAIRFIELD RD

Brewery

Fairfield

MAUMBURY RD

Police Station

Maumbury Rings

Warden's Post

York House
Stables

US Bakery & Canteen

CULLIFORD RD

Southern Railway

Station

ASHLEY RD

CROMWELL RD

ALFRED RD

MONMOUTH RD

Warden's Post

SOUTH COURT AVE

Free French Forces
Camp

Warden's Post

Lodge

Cemetery

G.W.R

Duffryn
Warden's Post HQ

MANOR RD

HERRINGSTON RD

Recreational
Ground
(The Rec)

Fire Fighting &
Gas Training Hut

Saw Mills

US Bakery

Brewery
Sports Ground

Isolation
Hospital

Defence against Invasion

⬡ Pillbox

■ Dragon's Teeth

● Wooden Poles

○ Holes in Road

Defence against Air Attacks

⊠ ARP Building

■ Air Raid Shelter

▶ Air Raid Siren

⎕ Static Water Tank

○ Searchlight/Anti Aircraft Guns

═ Trenches

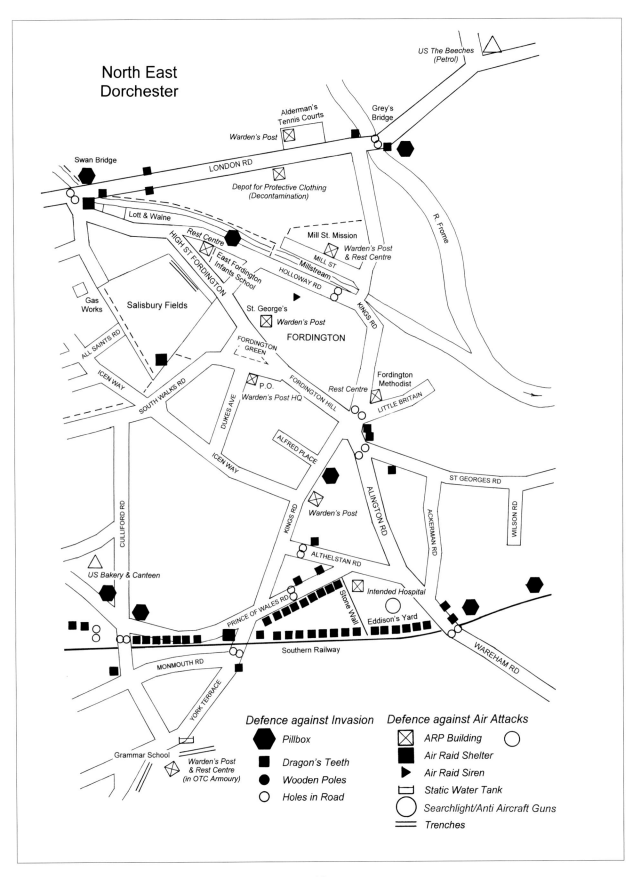

North East Dorchester

US The Beeches (Petrol)

Alderman's Tennis Courts

Grey's Bridge

Warden's Post

Swan Bridge

LONDON RD

Depot for Protective Clothing (Decontamination)

R. Frome

Lott & Walne

Rest Centre

Mill St. Mission

Warden's Post & Rest Centre

MILL ST

East Fordington Infants School

HIGH ST FORDINGTON

Millstream

HOLLOWAY RD

Gas Works

Salisbury Fields

KINGS RD

St. George's

Warden's Post

ALL SAINTS RD

FORDINGTON

ICEN WAY

FORDINGTON GREEN

SOUTH WALKS RD

DUKES AVE

P.O.

Warden's Post HQ

FORDINGTON HILL

Rest Centre

Fordington Methodist

LITTLE BRITAIN

CULLIFORD RD

ICEN WAY

ALFRED PLACE

ST GEORGES RD

ALINGTON RD

ACKERMAN RD

WILSON RD

KINGS RD

Warden's Post

US Bakery & Canteen

ALTHELSTAN RD

Intended Hospital

Stone Wall

Eddison's Yard

WAREHAM RD

PRINCE OF WALES RD

Southern Railway

MONMOUTH RD

YORK TERRACE

Grammar School

Warden's Post & Rest Centre (in OTC Armoury)

Defence against Invasion

⬢ Pillbox

■ Dragon's Teeth

● Wooden Poles

○ Holes in Road

Defence against Air Attacks

⊠ ARP Building   ○

■ Air Raid Shelter

▶ Air Raid Siren

⊔ Static Water Tank

○ Searchlight/Anti Aircraft Guns

═ Trenches

The lighthearted coat-of-arms drawn up for the Dorchester ARP
(Air Raid Precautions), based on the Borough Arms. The motto
suggests that the drawing was done in the early years of the war.

ONE

The Darkening Storm

Preparations for War

Although Great Britain's armed forces were quite unprepared for war when it eventually came in September 1939, much thought had already been given regarding the defence of the country against air attack.

As early as 1924 the Committee of Imperial Defence had begun considering the implications of a possible aerial war, and, in 1935, a Home Office department issued a circular to Dorset County Council requesting them to prepare plans to deal with all aspects of precautions against air raids.

Although many councils ignored the 'request', Dorset was one that complied and an Air Raid Precautions and Emergency Committee was set up in Dorchester in July 1936. Following this, Dorset was split into five groups, with Dorchester included in the Weymouth Area 2.

It was as well that they did so, as the Air Raid Wardens Service was created by the government in April 1937 and the original 'request' was then made compulsory. On 1 January 1938 police and local government began training in anti-gas measures. To cover Dorchester and district an ARP Controller was appointed, Capt L.C. Lyndon-Moore taking the post from inception to 1938 when he was succeeded by Mr Douglas Jackman MBE.

After the Munich crisis in 1938, Dorchester residents changed talking about 'if war comes' to 'when war comes' and there was a burst of activity. A 6d handbook entitled 'Personal Protection against Gas' sold out in Dorchester by the end of the first week of issue.

There was a large recruitment drive for ARP Wardens with both the Dorchester Plaza and Palace cinemas running film appeals, and posters appeared on the Town Pump, the Corn Exchange, and various hoardings throughout the town.

Wardens were to be 'mature and responsible persons', men over the age of thirty and women over twenty five. Even the BBC joined the campaign. In a 'Band-Wagon' variety show at the time 'Big-hearted' Arthur Askey and 'Stinker' Murdoch, referring to the 'mature and responsible' persons required, sang 'Big and Stinker must agree, now we've joined the A.R.P.' Appeals were also made to recruit into the Auxiliary Fire Service (AFS).

The Women's Voluntary Service for Civil Defence (WVS) was formed in May 1939, and was soon tirelessly working to protect families and help win a war should it occur. Their predominantly green uniforms were a familiar sight in Dorchester, and although the WVS was quickly referred to as 'Widows, Virgins and Spinsters' they were respected by all.

Another totally women's organisation was the Women's Institute, who never quite threw off their reputation of 'Jam and Jerusalem' but nevertheless did stoic work at a time when war seemed imminent. They and the Townswomen's Guild put in many long hours of hard work.

Yet another women's organisation was the Women's Land Army (WLA). In 1939 Miss Marsden, Chairwoman of the Dorset WLA, reminded employers that the Ministry of Agriculture and Fisheries had laid down that land girls over the age of 18 would receive £1 8s per week for a 48 hour week. Girls below that age would receive £1 2s 6d (this was equal to my first week's salary when I started work with Lloyds Bank in August 1944). The land girls were a popular sight in Dorchester with their green sweaters and dark brown dungarees, and they were often to be seen either at the Milk Bar in South Street or the Sun Inn, Charminster. In 1943 Rothesay House was bought and turned into a hostel for them.

In January 1939, following a broadcast by the Prime Minister, recruitment campaigns were stepped up – not only into the Armed Forces but also for Nursing, the Women's Land Army, Observer Corps and especially, Civil Defence.

Special Constables were recruited from men over the age of 20. Fit men over the age of 50, especially those connected to the building trade were needed for Rescue and Demolition Parties, while men from ages 30 to 50 and women from 18 to 50 were required as ambulance drivers. Men over the age of 45 and women over 18 were wanted to man the Report Centres.

Following on from the announcement of the Government's Evacuation Scheme and a poster campaign around Dorchester, the Dorchester Evacuation Committee announced that the borough was able to receive 1600 children, and the Town Clerk, Mr J. Adrian Hands, was detailed to organise their arrival. A reception area was set up at Maud Road School, with plans to provide each child with light refreshments together with a bag of food sufficient to last them two days.

My own first military memories relating to the war was watching, in 1938, a party of Army Royal Engineers constructing a 'bailey bridge' on the River Frome at Grey's Bridge. Once finished it was 'tested' by other troops: I think they were from the 94 (Queens Own Dorset Yeomanry) Field Regiment, who were staying in their headquarters at 57 High West Street at the time.

I can remember one soldier calling out to the interested civilian spectators, 'We will be using these to cross the Rhine one day'. How prophetic.

A Garrison Town

In 1939 Dorchester was the HQ for:

• 94th (QODY) Field Regiment – 57 High West Street – Commanding Officer Lt Col G.A. Pinney MC.

• Dorset Heavy Regiment – Commanding Officer Lt Col G.G.H. Symes OBE TD.

• 224th (Dorset) Field Battery (Dorchester Troop) – Maj C.B. Rumble.

• Dorset (Fortress) R E – Lt Col R.M. Dawes TD.

• 4th Battalion Dorsetshire Regiment –

Members of the Women's Land Army parading along High West Street in 1943.

Territorial Drill Hall, Poundbury Road – Lt Col D. Baxter MC.

• HQ Company, 4th Battalion Dorsetshire Regiment.

In early 1939 there was a local recruitment drive on behalf of the 94th (Dorset and Hampshire) Field Regiment, Royal Artillery. Their official history, published after the war, records that a few days after the declaration of war the Regiment moved to Wilton in Wiltshire. One has visions of a convoy of Army trucks filled with soldiers and towing their guns. Not quite the picture one recruit recalls. There was a dearth of both guns and towing vehicles (the Regiment only had one usable truck at the time!). The one 18 pounder gun that there was was towed by local coal merchant

Officers of the 1st Battalion, Dorsetshire Regiment, outside the Depot Barracks in 1939. The Regiment played a distinguished part in the war, taking part in the landings in Sicily, Italy and Normandy. The 1st Battalion landed early on D-Day, and formed part of the first infantry patrol to cross into Germany.

Joe Whitty's coal lorry. To make matters worse, the gun lacked a firing pin so couldn't have been fired. The troops themselves went by local buses and Wood's Furniture vehicles.

The 94th had a distinguished war record and on Saturday 11th November 1944 became the first field gun force to cross into Germany, being part of the Anglo-American drive into the Geilenkirchen area.

Many firms had their vehicles requisitioned, amongst them Thurmans, Ironmongers, who lost their fleet of country delivery vans to the Army. One was later spotted in France with 'Thurmans' still decipherable on its side panel. As late as 1941 Joe Whitty's lorries were still transporting soldiers to rifle ranges.

Exercises Begin

Prime Minister Chamberlain agreed to conscription in April 1939. War with Germany suddenly seemed inevitable. Dorchester responded with a flurry of activity. Residents were advised that gas masks (officially called Respirators) for the town were now available, and given the name and address of the Distribution Depots from which they were to be collected should the necessity arise.

For ARP purposes, the town had been divided into five zones and it was essential that gas masks were collected from the correct location. Living in Monmouth Road, our Distribution Depot was the Boys Grammar School. We were also told that we would have to sign for the masks and hand in the white ARP cards, already issued. Later on, after their collection, every household in the town was visited by its local ARP warden and shown how to wear them.

Although everyone believed the Germans would use gas and there was a very real fear of how we would react, the subject was not without humour, and I well remember joining in the singing of a parody of the then popular song 'Under the Spreading Chestnut Tree'. Referring to the then Prime Minister, Neville Chamberlain, the parody was 'Under the Spreading Chestnut Tree, Neville Chamberlain said to me, If you want to get your gas mask free, join the blooming ARP'. Not true however, as gas masks were later issued free of charge. Perhaps because we were so well prepared for a gas attack, Hitler never used it against the civilian population.

Also in April, Dorchester experienced its first 'blackout' exercise. It was planned to start at 11.20 p.m., on the grounds that pubs and the cinema would have closed and most people would be at home. All street lighting was to be turned off, all house and business premises to be blacked out, and vehicles to be driven with side lights only.

The exercise also featured an imaginary air raid resulting in a mustard bomb being dropped in North Square. The Fire Brigade were assisted by Boy Scouts as messengers, and pumps were also

Air Raid Precautions, Dorchester.

Gas Masks for the Civil Population of Dorchester are now in store in the town, and will be issued in case of emergency only.

If the necessity for distribution does arise, it may have to be carried out quickly, therefore the co-operation of the inhabitants in the following arrangements is earnestly requested.

For A.R.P. purposes the town is divided into five Zones. The Masks will be distributed from one Depot in each Zone, as shown overleaf. Each Depot will be supplied with the correct number of Masks for the Zone, **the Public are therefore** requested to take careful **note of the Depot to which they should go.** When collecting their Masks, the Public will be requested to sign for them, **and to hand in the White A.R.P. Cards already issued.**

The sizes of Masks available are large, medium and small. Masks for those children who would take the infant's size will be available later.

Sick and aged people unable to go to the Depots will have their Masks delivered as quickly as possible. After the issue of Masks every house will be visited by a Warden, who will, if desired, check the fittings. Any resident not in possession of a White Card can be fitted for a Mask and obtain a Card from the Warden who delivers this notice.

Any further information can be obtained from the A.R.P.O., 21, North Square.

Information about the supply of gas masks and a list of the various depots from where they could be collected, issued in April 1939 when war suddenly seemed unavoidable.

Distributing Depots for Gas Masks.

ZONE A. Distributing Depot Dorford Baptist Schoolroom.	ZONE B. Distributing Depot Park Mission Cambridge Road.	ZONE C. Distributing Depot Mill Street Mission.	ZONE D. Distributing Depot Grammar School.	ZONE E. Distributing Depot Corn Exchange.	
ROADS.	ROADS.	ROADS.	ROADS.	ROADS.	ROADS.
Bridport Road	Alice Road	Alfred Place	Ashley Road	Acland Road	High East Street
Gloucester Road	Alexandra Road	Athelstan Road	Amphitheatre	All Saints Road	High West Street
Hawthorne Road	Cambridge Road	Alington Road	Terrace	Alexandra Terrace	Icen Way (Central
Mountain Ash	Coburg Road	Ackerman Road	Alfred Road	Albert Road	Ward)
Road	Clarence Road	Alington Avenue	Cromwell Road	Alington Street	Linden Avenue
Prospect Road	Damers Road	Dukes Avenue	Culliford Road	Castle Row	Millers Close
Poundbury Farm	Dagmar Road	Fordington Green	Herringston Road	Colliton Street	Maumbury Road
Poundbury Road	Edward Road	Gordon Terrace	Manor Road	Cornhill	North Square
St. Thomas Road	Florence Road	Hardy Avenue	Monmouth Road	Church Street	Northernhay
Middle Farm	Garfield Avenue	Holloway Road	Prince of Wales	Charles Street	Orchard Street
	Lorne Road	High Street,	Road	Cornwall Road	Princes Street
	Louise Road	Fordington	Railway Cottages	D. C. Hospital	Salisbury Street
	Marie Road	Hillside Terrace	Rothesay Road	(Staff)	& Walks
	Milford Road	Icen Way (East	South Court	Durngate Street	Somerleigh Road
	Maud Road	Ward)	Avenue	Friary Hill	South Walks
	Maiden Castle	Kings Road	York Road	Friary Lane	South Street
	Farm	London Road	York Terrace	Frome Terrace	St. Helens Road
	Maiden Castle	Little Britain		The Grove	Trinity Street
	Road	Louds Mill		Greenings Court	Victoria Road
	Olga Road	Mill Street		Grey School	Wollaston Road
	Queens Avenue	Pound Lane		Passage	West Walks
	Treves Road	South Walks Road		Greyhound Yard	Weymouth
	Windsor Road	(from Fordington		Glyde Path Road	Avenue
	Weymouth	Green to Icen Way)		Great Western	(Town side of Bridge)
	Avenue	Syward Road		Road	
	(beyond Bridge)	St. Georges Road			
		Vicarage Lane			
		Victoria Terrace			
		Wilson Road			

PLEASE GO TO YOUR CORRECT DEPOT.   Keep this notice with your other **A.R.P.** literature.   P.T.O.

sent to the top of Damers Road and another to Little Britain. One interesting result was the number of people who, after the exercise had finished, reported still being able to smell the mustard gas: they were quite mistaken as at no time had any mustard gas been used!

The *Dorset Daily Echo* reported 'many loopholes', in that large areas of the town had not heard the air raid siren as the wind had been blowing in the wrong direction. Mistakes had occurred at the Report Centre, and there had been a lack of sufficient messengers. According to the *Echo,* the co-operation of householders 'left much to be desired'. Traffic signals had been too brilliantly lit and the whole exercise had been severely curtailed because of the bad weather – a decision much regretted later as many of the defence systems had not been tested at all. Even the police came in for criticism – they had shown 'excessive zeal which must not happen again'. Reading between the lines of both the Official Report and the *Echo*, the whole exercise was a complete fiasco.

Other exercises did follow. One was an 'air raid' between 11 p.m. and midnight whose 'casualties' were taken to a base hospital and the British Red Cross hut in Icen Way, with first aid given in the Mayor's parlour. Members of the local VAD/4 and St John's Ambulance co-operated with ARP personnel. Umpires included Messrs J. Adrian Hands, A.C. Templeman and J. Wilson. The outcome of this exercise is not recorded.

Early in 1939, each household in Dorchester received a 36-page booklet entitled *The Protection of your House against Air Raids*. Beginning in July there was a further flurry of leaflets, the one on Civil Defence including such subjects as 'If War Comes', 'Lighting Restrictions', and 'Evacuation'. A second leaflet contained instructions regarding gas masks and masking windows, whilst another was called *Your Food in Wartime*.

At the same time public information leaflets were available covering a variety of subjects. For 2d you could buy *The Organisation of Air Raid Casualties, Rescue Parties* and the *Clearing of Debris*, whilst 5d bought the organisation of *Decontamination Services, Air Raid Wardens* and *Anti-Gas Training*.

Notices began appearing in shop windows advising residents where they could obtain protective oilskin clothing: the nearest stockist was a firm in the Old Kent Road, London. Boots the Chemist advertised a large selection of first aid equipment as well as 'Medical and Surgical Requisites which could be useful in the preparation of a gas protection room'. Other shops offered rubber waterproof torches at 5/- each and an ARP torch for hand and belt for 5/3d.

In June, Oswald Mosley, leader of the British Fascists, gave an address in the Corn Exchange on the advantages of Fascism. Even after the declaration of war, early in 1940, the authorities permitted the British Fascists to hold an open meeting in Maumbury Rings. The speakers were R. Saunders and T. Cosson, accompanied as usual by their Fascist bodyguard. Fights broke out when many in the audience, mostly servicemen, attempted to wreck the loudspeaker, and the meeting was hastily abandoned.

On 3 August Dorchester RDC decreed 'In view of the imminent outbreak of war that the whole power of the Council so far allowed by law, be delegated to an Emergency Committee until further notice'. A Police War Department was set up and a War Cabinet established, to deal with all matters at twelve hours' notice.

Ten days later, shortly after midnight, the air-raid siren was again tested. Councillor Freddie James who only lived 200 yards from the siren, slept through it – as did many living on the outskirts of town.

On 24 August, the Emergency Powers (Defence) Act was passed. Military reservists were called up, and ARP Wardens told to 'stand by'. Since the mistakes made during the blackout exercise in April both residents and Civil Defence personnel had been given ample training and instruction. Residents were reminded that 'even the light of a candle can be seen from a length of 2 miles on a clear night'. We were very gullible in those days, even believing that by eating carrots our night-time vision would be greatly enhanced.

On September 1, blackout was officially brought in. All street lighting and illuminated signs were switched off, windows and doors 'blacked out' and car headlights masked, leaving only a small area

A Civil Defence Gas Decontamination Squad on exercise outside the entrance to Dorchester Prison in North Square, April 1941.

exposed (known locally as 'Chinese slits'). Buses had their windows painted over inside the bus, which meant that one could not see where one's 'stop' was. At night any house that showed even a glimmer of light received a visit from an ARP warden, and prosecution followed for perpetual offenders. We became quite disorientated, and there were reports in the *Echo* of people falling into the sea at nearby Weymouth (and no, they were not drunk at the time).

Also on the 1st September, the Dorchester Borough Surveyor, Mr H.G. Strange, called for volunteers to fill sand bags. Twenty four people including schoolboys from the Boys Grammar, Colliton and Senior Schools turned up and used 150 tons of sand to fill 5000 sacks. This took place at the DCC Yard, Poundbury, with refreshments provided by local households and the YMCA mobile canteen. The sandbags were later distributed around houses, business premises and public buildings. Incidentally, the price of sandbags rose from 2¾d in June 1939 to 5d in September.

That same Friday the first children evacuees arrived by train from London. Four hundred girls and boys crowded the platform of the GWR station, before walking in crocodile to the Girls Council School in Victoria Park. Here they were greeted by the Dorchester Reception and Billeting Committee, helped by members of the Dorchester Red Cross, VAD and British Legion. Their ages ranged from 5 to 14 and all carried a small attaché case, their gas masks and a name label attached to their clothes. They also carried a franked postcard to be sent to their parents notifying them of their new address. They were served light refreshments, given bags of food sufficient for two days, divided into groups for billets, and taken to their new homes. Although the actual arrival, reception and dispersal went well, there were several hiccups between individual evacuees and those with whom they were billeted. The billeting allowance was 8/6 per evacuee per week.

The *Echo* announced in its 1st September

Dorchester First Aid Post Centre, which once the German bombing offensive began was manned every day in case of raids. An early casualty was a Mr Weolmsley Lewis, an architect, who arrived suddenly and said he had been badly bitten by a horse.

edition that congratulations were due to the ARP authorities on completion of all Dorchester residents having been measured for their gas mask. Everyone had been issued with a registration card detailing their name, address and size of mask. After assembly and distribution to the relative pick-up points, all that was required was to present the card at the appropriate point, collect the mask and sign for its issue. The report concluded by naming Mr D. Jackman as the Borough ARP Officer.

The ARP was mobilised on the 1st September and on the 2nd September the County Emergency Committee (CEC) held their first meeting at Dorchester, reporting on arrangements made to bring the county air raid precautions into immediate effect. As far as Dorchester itself was concerned the following were confirmed:

1. A Report Centre to be set up at 21 North Square, the entrance to be protected by sandbags and a blast wall. The Centre would include a telephone, liaison and controller's room, protected sleeping accommodation for one shift and a store room. The Centre was to cost £625 and would be responsible for co-ordinating the receipt of messages from the wardens and calling out other services to assist them. Ever-conscious of expense – even at the start of a war – the CEC reported that the rent would be £10 a year and the rent of garages for two ambulances £2.8s per month and a garage for two private cars £1 per month.

ARP HQ was later transferred to the basement in County Hall and large blast walls were built outside.

The equivalent for the Dorchester Rural District Council was set up at No 56 High West Street in a room over Stickland & Rendall, Ladies & Gents hairdressers. They soon moved to premises at No 27 over Lee Motor Works (Bournemouth) Ltd.

2. Rescue Depots for the storage of vehicles and equipment required for rescuing trapped casualties, the shoring up of buildings in imminent danger of collapse and demolishing dangerous structures created by bombing. These were in the Borough Corporation Yard at the Top O'Town and in the south block of The Shire Hall.

3. Fixed First Aid Points where lightly wounded could be treated and the more serious casualties referred on to hospital. This would be at the County Clinic in Glyde Path Road.

4. Decontamination and Cleansing Centre (Personnel). This was for the cleansing of streets, buildings and other structures which had been contaminated by poison gas. To be constructed in the Borough Corporation Yard at Top O'Town at a cost of £1005.

5. Public Gas Clearing Station to be sited in the Fairfield Market.

In due course the town was also be provided with the following:

- **4 Road Party Depots.**
- **7 Ambulance Centres.** Later, on 1 March 1940, permission was received from the Ministry of Health to purchase three converted vehicles for use as ambulances.
- **5 First Aid Posts**. First Aid parties were in the charge of Mr Sid Stevens (dentist) and Mr Clark (chemist) with their depot in the Top O'Town car park. Other personnel included Mr Jack Skyrme (Thurmans), Mr Percy Thomas, Mr Jack Thomas (Tilleys Motors) in charge of transport – this was private cars for sitting casualties and an ambulance carrying four stretchers. Each had a five man crew on duty (one night a week) and another on standby. They trained with the Home Guard every Sunday.
- **2 Decontamination Squads.** Authority was received on 24th November 1939 to purchase 1000 suits of underclothing from Jackmans of Dorchester at a cost not exceeding 5/- per suit for use by Decontamination personnel.
- **1 Detached Rescue Section.**
- **2 Rescue Parties.**

Wardens' Posts

A Warden Service had already been set up, manned by people with an intimate knowledge of an area and it was their duty to report initial damage, obtain help and act as a help to residents in their particular locality.

For Dorchester the following Wardens' posts had been set up:
- HQ The Sydney Arms, Bridport Road: known as Windy Corner (*see photograph on following page*) (though after 1942 it moved further along the Bridport Road to the Laundry – a move probably not appreciated by those concerned!)
- HQ Herridge's Yard, with posts at Durngate, Clarence Road and Cemetery Lodge.
- HQ Fordington Post Office, with posts at Mill Street Mission, Aldermans' Tennis Courts, Fordington Green and Kings Road.
- HQ Duffryn, Herringston Road, with posts at Monmouth Road, York House Stables, Prince of Wales Road, Dorchester Grammar School (in the school OTC Armoury building).
- HQ Friary Press, with posts at 1 West Walks, Loders Garage, Borough Library (next to Fire Station).

A later warden's post was set up in dentist Mr Sid Steven's house at the Top O'Town, High West Street. Sandbags were piled up inside the railings facing onto High West Street and up both sides of the window. The Queen's Avenue area wardens used the wooden hut at the cemetery gates on Weymouth Avenue. Later they were told to report for duty only if the sirens sounded, but they often heard the Weymouth sirens first.

Rest centres were set up at the County School for Girls and the Senior School in Coburg Road; the Council School in Maud Road; Dorchester Grammar School, Culliford Road; School for Girls, Icen Way; East Fordington Infants School, Holloway Road; West Fordington Infants School, The Grove; The Boys School, Colliton Street; the Mill Street Mission, Mill Street; and the Wesleyan Mission Hall at Fordington Cross.

Six Gas Identification Officers were appointed to cover the borough. Specialists, with a science or chemical background, their principal task was to identify what type of gas had been used if an attack took place. One of the six was 'Ticker' Cole, the

WINDY CORNER POST, 1942

Science master at Dorchester Grammar School.

On 24th Nov 1939 the DCC decreed that all essential ARP buildings were to be sandbagged by voluntary labour. The only ones I can remember seeing sandbagged were those at the ARP HQ in North Square.

Military Hospital

To provide for the expected influx of wounded servicemen plans were put forward for building a military hospital in Prince of Wales' Road. The wounded would be ferried from France to Weymouth and onward by train to Dorchester. Plans were made for a siding to enter the hospital grounds from the main Weymouth to Waterloo railway line (as there was at next door Eddisons). This was never completed. In the event, building work did not commence until after the war and the

The ARP Wardens' Post at 'Windy Corner' outside the Sydney Arms, Bridport Road, 1942, including Ernie Wills, Jack Tarr and Joe Whitefield. All carry gas masks, and note the stirrup pump in the foreground and protective strips on the windows.

hospital was never used as such but occupied by the Dorset WAEC. Even today the front of the building looks like a hospital entrance.

Fire Brigade

Who can forget the fire station in Trinity Street with its red concertina front doors and the always well-polished Dennis fire engines inside? In the early days of the war the fire vehicles were supplemented with private cars fitted with tow-bars on which they hitched Coventry Climax trailers with fire pumps. There was a garage in

Cromwell Road where a trailer pump was kept and towed by Mr Bob Watts (he had a motorcycle shop in South Street). Another was in Linden Avenue (long since demolished to make way for flats) and members of the AFS would meet there, amongst them Mr Reg Grant, Mr 'Hammer' Gill and Mr Freddie Shiner (other firemen at the time were Mr 'Dusty' Miller and Mr Jack Hodder).

Dorchester Fire Brigade at the beginning of the war. The vehicle on the left was a Morris Oxford car converted to carry a 50 foot escape ladder. The Leyland fire engine next to it was already 13 years old when the photograph was taken. The Morris tender on the right usually towed the Dennis trailer pump alongside it.

TWO

War is Declared

Most Dorchester people I talked to whilst compiling this book complained of some memory loss, but everyone could remember where they were and what they were doing on the day war was declared. It was a sunny Sunday in Dorchester when the BBC announced at 10 a.m. on September 3rd 1939 that the Prime Minister would speak to the nation at 11.15 a.m..

Neville Chamberlain duly spoke from No 10 Downing Street: 'This morning the British Ambassador in Berlin handed the German government a final note, stating that unless the British government heard from them by 11 o'clock that they were prepared to withdraw their troops from Poland, a state of war would exist between us. I have to tell you that no such undertaking has been received, and that consequently this country is at war with Germany.'

The announcement was followed by the playing of the National Anthem, and I expect most Dorchester families did as ours did – silently standing until it had finished.

Although the announcement was widely expected, there was still a sense of shock to actually hear it. The news was met with mixed feelings, of which the most overriding was a sense of relief that a decision had been taken after months of uncertainty. Suddenly, we all knew where we stood. After the German annexation of Austria in 1938, the occupation of Czechoslovakia in March 1939, followed finally by the invasion of Poland on September 1st, most British people felt that 'enough was enough' and the time had come to face up to Germany. 'We'll show old Hitler where to get off' was the general theme, with the optimists declaring, 'It will all be over by Christmas'.

Being young, I was a bit bewildered by it all, but I remember my father, who had served as an NCO with the Dorsetshire Regiment during World War I, took a more sober view, remembering the death and destruction that war brings, whatever the final outcome. My mother's main concern seemed to be her ability to feed the family once food rationing started. Naturally no one knew what would happen next, but there was a general fear of gas being used by Hitler against the civilian population. Why else had the Government issued every man, woman and child, with a gas mask?

At 4.30 in the afternoon the BBC announced that all places of entertainment would be closed until further notice, and that all schools in an evacuation area (and that included Dorchester) would be shut for at least a week. Banks and the Stock Exchange would not re-open until the Tuesday. It also advised people to keep off the streets as much as possible and to carry their gas masks.

At 6 p.m. King George VI broadcast to the nation: 'In this grave hour, perhaps the most fateful in our history, I send to every household of my people, both at home and overseas, this message – for the sake of all that we ourselves hold dear and of the world's order and peace, it is unthinkable that we should refuse to meet the challenge.' He finished with, 'To this high purpose, I now call my people at home and my people across the sees. I ask them to stand firm and united in this hour of trial.'

The same day the National Service (Armed Forces) Act was passed by parliament whereby all fit men aged 18-41 were liable for military service. This was extended to include women in 1941, and also increased the age limit for men to 51. All this was accepted but there was genuine disagreement when, in July 1943, all women aged 46-50 were required to register for War Work – 'Grannies Call Up' , as it was dubbed.

In Dorchester, young men had to register at Top O'Town House on their sixteenth birthday in order to be 'called up'. The *Echo* reported on 5th September that 'Under the National Registration Bill there was a call for registration of all persons in the UK except members of the Armed Forces'. Young people, who wished to, could join the Boy Scouts, Girl Guides and Boys Brigade. In February 1941 the Air Training Corps was formed, and in 1942, the Sea Cadet Corps and the Army Cadet Corps.

Following the Declaration of War the whole of Dorchester seemed to be 'on the move' – regular servicemen reporting back to their HQ, reservists and territorials making for their respective report centres, in addition to all the civilian movements – nurses, firemen, civil service personnel etc.

I remember on Monday September 4th going into town with my mother to queue outside endless shops. People seemed determined to stock up with everything and anything, whether they needed it or not. Only the banks remain closed in order to complete the arrangements for adapting themselves to the emergency, re-opening the following day.

The Headquarters of the Dorsetshire Regiment, The Keep, on the Bridport Road. The photograph was probably taken shortly after war was declared in September 1939. Note the sentry, and the fact that the A343 road sign has not yet been taken down to impede any German advance. The Marabout gun is just visible in the background.

Directives and Orders

Also on September 4th lists of directives and orders appeared in both the national and local newspapers. I have listed them under various headings but four that did not come under any general heading were:

Doctors. Those enrolled under the Ministry of Health emergency service and who have been asked to report for duty at a specified hospital at the outset of an emergency should now report accordingly.

Milk is to be delivered to householders once a day and in daylight.

Mortgages. Men called up for active service need not fear that when they return the houses they have built on borrowed money will be lost. Parliament has decreed that so long as interest is paid on borrowed capital there can be no foreclosure. Interest cannot be increased.

Identification. Make sure that you and every member of your household, especially children, have on them, their names and address clearly written. Do this either on something like a luggage label, not an odd piece of paper which might be lost. Sew the label on to your children's clothing.

Then followed a long list of things not to do under the large capital letter heading DON'T:

'DON'T listen to rumours – all the news, good or bad, will be in the newspapers – disbelieve everything else you hear.

DON'T broadcast information – you may know there is an AA gun cunningly concealed in the field next to your garden – that's no reason for passing on the information. It may reach someone who should not know it.

DON'T lose your head – in other words 'keep smiling'. Nothing can be gained by going about with the corners of your mouth turned down and it has a bad effect on people whose nerves are not as good as yours.

DON'T listen to scaremongers. Just treat them as you would a smallpox case – move on quickly. The enemy loves to spread rumours. Part of his campaign is to panic.

DON'T cause crowds to assemble. If you see people gathering, walk on. In other words 'Mind your own business'.

Be silent, be discreet, enemy ears are listening to you. Now get ahead, do your job and don't worry.'

Aliens

A notice appeared in the *Dorset Daily Echo* informing its readers that under the Aliens Act all persons providing lodging for reward must complete a form, the only exception being members of the Armed Forces, in uniform.

Aliens were required to register and long queues formed outside the Police HQ in Weymouth Avenue. Those who were considered to be a threat to national security were interned for the duration of the war, the rest were required to report regularly to the Police Station.

Conscientous Objectors

In the early days of the War there was much ill-feeling against people who refused to fight for their country – 'conchies' as they were referred to. Some Dorchester ladies decided to form a 'white feather' group and a white feather – the traditional sign for cowardice – was given to those who refused to fight for their country.

Evacuation

After the initial influx of 400 evacuated children on the 1st September, more continued to arrive daily. Not everyone welcomed them, and the members of the County Emergency Committee made their feelings clear at a meeting on the following day: 'We strongly protest against the London City Council billeting scheme for evacuated families who have been sent unexpectedly to this area, and billeted on county families regardless of the difficulties in standards of living and of the unsurmountable difficulties occasioned by forcibly overcrowding county homes with the result that many families have returned to London. We suggest an alternative scheme that the Authority responsible take over empty homes and buildings and recondition them, to take the families'.

As early as September 4, the day after the Declaration, articles appeared in the newspapers relating to the feeding of evacuees. Under the headline 'Economical Feeding', and alongside an idyllic picture of two well-scrubbed evacuee children being offered food by a well-dressed lady against a background of open countryside (complete with singing bird perched on a branch), the article started by saying that 'many housewives are now facing the problem of catering for evacuated children. Recipes have to be economical but also provide satisfying health-giving food to growing youngsters. It is no easy task'. It went on to remind readers that children in a strange home amongst strange people are apt to be a little off their food, so they must be humoured and given food that is attractive and varied. The article went on to give examples, including potato soup, liver casserole ('particularly good for slightly anaemic children'), baked marrow, blackberry bake and golden apples.

Amongst the child evacuees to Dorchester were the Rains family: (from left to right) John, Kenneth, Christine, Bernard and Kathleen.

On the same day the newspapers carried reminders to the parents of evacuated children that 'Parents must on no account go to see their children until they are told to do so'. It was explained that they might not be able to return the same day and it was very unlikely that any accommodation could be found for them.

On September 7, Dorchester residents were warned that those with whom children were billeted must not 'swap' them with other children billeted elsewhere in the town. 'Swopping' evacuees was an offence, and the Town Clerk, Mr J. Adrian Hands, announced his intention to prosecute persistent offenders.

At the time, the Government glossed over the many difficulties that were encountered, but there were very real problems. The main complaint was one of hygiene, or rather the lack of it. Bed wetting and head lice were common. Many children were filthy, verminous, and lacking any idea of cleanliness. Their clothes were shabby, many wore shoes without soles. One complaint, often heard once parental visits were allowed, was that the evacuees parents were no better behaved. The NSPCC were often called to assist and there were many reports containing such phrases as 'the house has been completely wrecked', 'appalling condition', 'the children are filthy and suffer from rickets', 'the parents have no control over their children'. Often Dorchester families were compensated and in all severe cases the evacuees were returned to London.

The real problem was a complete clash of ways of life – Dorchester's children heard the 'F' word for the first time, and discovered that some Londoners prefer to eat fish and chips whilst sitting on the door step or pavement rather than sitting around the kitchen table for a family meal. Many of the evacuees had never seen a cow before and thought milk came from bottles. Many, including their parents, were bored and homesick and quickly returned to London. By January 1940, 75% of the evacuees had returned to London, pointing out that the reasons for their evacuation – the fear of air raids on the city – had not materialised.

Soldiers were billeted in Dorchester throughout the war, particularly after Dunkirk. These two soldiers were No 9 Commando, and were billeted in Queen's Avenue in October 1942. One carries a Lee Enfield .303 rifle, the other has an American Thompson sub-machine gun (Tommy gun) slung over his shoulder.

For those that stayed, the evacuee payment was 10/6 for each unaccompanied child and 8/6 if more than one. In March 1940 it was decided to set up a special centre for incontinent or difficult evacuees at a building called 'Langdon' in Prince of Wales Road, the centre to be used by all local authorities in Dorset who had problem evacuees.

In May 1941 the centre was visited by the Childrens Homes Sub Committee of the Public Assistance Committee, whose report was critical – mainly due to the different types of children admitted. It July it was decided that 'Langdon' would be better managed by the Caldecott Community.

In March 1943 the CEC reported there were 250 evacuees, composed almost entirely of unaccompanied children, still billeted in Dorchester. There was no systematic visiting of their temporary wartime homes, but teachers' reports suggesting a visit was necessary were followed up by the County Welfare Officer or a member of the billeting staff. In February 1945 the majority of the remaining evacuees boarded a train for London, and the last group of children had gone by July.

Although the criticisms are well documented, the evacuation scheme worked adequately in Dorchester. Some of the children were as young as five, and one can only sympathise when considering how bewildered and frightened they must have been to be suddenly taken away from familiar surroundings and packed off to live with strangers.

Also evacuated to Dorchester was the Haberdasher Aske School from Acton. This was an all-girls school and they shared the Dorset County School for Girls in Coburg Road (the Green School); the Green School girls using the classrooms in the mornings and the visitors in the afternoon. It must be said that they were not enthusiastically welcomed by the Green School girls, who accused their visitors of being rather superior and looking down on their country bumpkins. There were also rather unkind remarks about their cloche hats! On their eventual return to London some teachers stayed on, including Stella Evans, an art teacher, who joined the staff of Dorchester Grammar School.

Later, another school, the Caldicott School, was also evacuated to Dorchester, as was another Acton school, Rothschild Junior School. They used the classrooms of Colliton Street School in the afternoons of one week and on the mornings of the following week. Later they made use of the Dorchester YMCA building in Icen Way.

Although the need for evacuation was accepted, many wondered why Dorchester had been chosen to receive them. After all, it was only a few miles inland from the coast, where enemy troops might easily land if the threatened invasion took place. Later it was included in a Regulated Defence Area as a military town near to the ports of Weymouth and Portland and the nearby Warmwell Aerodrome – all liable to air attack.

Billeting

Although the taking in of evacuees was voluntary, billeting was compulsory. After conscription was introduced in 1939, many recruits were sent to Dorchester Barracks to complete their basic training, receiving instruction from officers and non-commissioned officers of The Dorsetshire Regiment. The barracks were unable to cope with such large numbers so many were billeted in public buildings and private houses. Amongst them were the Trinity Street Garage, next to what is now the Trinity Street entrance to Antelope Walk, the Dorford Baptist Church Sunday School Hall, and both the Recreation Ground and Football Ground in Weymouth Avenue.

Families with a spare room were obliged to have troops billeted on them and received 27/- per soldier, per week. As well as those doing their basic training, men of both No 4 and No 9 Commando were billeted on the town. My parents had two commandos billeted on them and as a schoolboy I still remember the excitement of seeing them arrive back after a hard day's training, in their distinctive green berets, toggle ropes around their shoulders, and carrying rifles or 'tommy guns'. I also remember their ravenous appetites! They were such good company, and always cheerful. We used to go down to the River Frome, along Frome Terrance, and watch them having 'piggy-back' races in the river.

In a report by the CEC to the Dorset County Council in May 1941 it was reported that at that time 25,000 troops were billeted in the county in private houses, halls and requisitioned houses, in addition to military camps – but I have been unable to find out how many of them were actually billeted in Dorchester.

For boarding soldiers, Dorchester publicans received 10d a night to include an evening meal and 8d for each additional soldier. To provide breakfast, the publican would receive 8d, for dinner 11d, tea 3d, and supper 1/-.

For officers the payment made was 3/- (not including food) and 2/- for each additional officer. In addition – and remarkably in a war dependent on tanks and artillery – a boarding fee of 2/3d was paid for a horse, to include a stable, 10lbs oats, 12lbs hay and 8lbs straw each day.

T.A. Webb of Webb, Major & Co, Timber and Builders' merchants, wearing his gas mask. Mr Webb initially served with the Observer Corps, but because they only had two or three rifles he joined the Home Guard.

Respirators (Gas Masks)

On the day after the war broke out we were advised that if poison gas were to be used, we would be warned by hand rattles. We were to keep off the streets and remain in our shelters until the gas had been cleared away. This would be indicated by hand bells.

On September 13, Miss P.C. Ruegg, Headmistress of the Dorset County School for Girls (The Green School) organised her staff and pupils to help distribute 14,000 gas masks. They had been assembled by prisoners in Dorchester Prison in their spare time. Each mask, which smelt disgustingly of rubber (hardly surprising as that was what they were made of !) was contained in a cardboard box with sufficient string attached to be carried from the shoulder.

Naturally, many ladies soon made more fashionable bags 'to look better'. The *Echo* observed that some people had been seen carrying their gas masks in small knapsacks, others in cases similar to camera cases, whilst cyclists often placed theirs on their carrier or in their baskets. They had also noticed that businessmen, often rather subconsciously, would either tuck them under an arm or dangle them from one finger. Ladies used them to double-up as a handbag and carry lipsticks and powder etc in them. Young children were issued with 'Mickey Mouse' gas masks and parents were encouraged to play games with the masks in order that their offspring would not be frightened should gas be dropped. Babies under the age of about 2½ years of age were issued with anti-gas protective helmets.

Posters urging people to carry gas masks appeared, bearing such phrases as, 'Take care of your gas mask and it will take care of you'. The first to appear was one issued by the Ministry of Home Security: 'Hitler will send no warning – so always carry your gas mask.'

In March 1940 the Ministry announced that schoolchildren were no longer required to carry their respirators every day, but respirator drill would be held at their school one day a month. A year later, with the Blitz now underway, the Ministry changed its mind and decreed that 'all schoolchildren will carry their respirator daily'! Most people did take advice against gas attacks seriously and some even went as far as making one room of their house gas proof, usually with the use of cellulose sheets and tape.

The Borough Council gave the top of each pillar box in the town a coating of yellowish-green gas detector paint.

There was an inspection of respirators on an October Sunday in 1943. Residents were required to take their gas masks to designated places: Wardens Post A1, the Steam Laundry, Post D2, Wheeler's Garage, Monmouth Road, Post D4, the Armoury, Dorchester Grammar School. Also to Maud Road School, the Magistrates' Court, Corn Exchange, and Moule Institute Fordington Hill. Children's respirators were inspected at school, but baby helmets and Mickey Mouse respirators had to be taken to the First Aid Post, County Clinic in Glyde Path Road on Tuesday and Friday afternoons.

The Blackout

Apart from the new wartime regulations and restrictions our lives were affected in countless minor ways. The traditional bonfire and firework displays on Guy Fawkes Night proved a very 'damp squib', as both bonfires and fireworks were banned (many parents looked upon this as a blessing in disguise).

Midnight church services on Christmas Eve were also cancelled in all Dorchester churches because of the difficulties churches had in blacking out their large stained-glass windows. Carol singers were unable to ring hand bells and even football supporters suffered by being unable to cheer on Dorchester Town Football Club, as rattles were also banned. These were covered by a Defence Regulation brought in by the Ministry of Information in September whereby it was forbidden to sound 'within public hearing any siren, hooter, whistle, rattle, bell, horn, gong or similar instrument except in accordance with directions for air raid warning purposes'. No church bells were to be rung during the war, as they were only to be rung to notify the start of the expected invasion. There was one exception, for they were rung on November 15 1942 to celebrate 'Monty's' victory at El Alamein in North Africa).

The most inconvenient and generally disliked restriction was undoubtedly the blackout. As the centrepiece of the Government's air raid precautions, it affected everyone – pedestrian, cyclist, householder, vehicle driver, visitor. No one escaped. Blackout curtain material sold in Dorchester shops at 1/- per yard, two yards wide. Some enterprising housewives lined them with bright and cheerful materials. Thick blankets or brown paper stretched on wooden frames were used to cover doors and sky lights and lavatory windows were painted over. Drawing pins became scarce overnight.

As early as September Dorchester residents were rather sarcastically reminded by the *Echo* that many had obviously not realised that blackout regulations were compulsory! Motorists were reminded that they must not switch on their garage lights whilst putting their cars away. Householders were told that it was forbidden to use shaded lights behind yellow blinds. All were reminded that failure to comply with blackout regulations could result in imprisonment for 3 months or a fine of £500, or both. The blackout extended from half an hour after sunset to half an hour before sunrise, which the day after the war broke out was 7.40 in the evening. Summer time was extended further by the introduction of Double Summer Time.

Motorists and cyclists came in for special reminders. The former were told that if the air-raid warning sounded whilst driving at night they were to pull in and park and turn off their engines. Headlights were to be switched off but rear side lights left on. Valuables had to be removed and all occupants proceed to the nearest shelter (later in 1941 a new traffic law was passed which made it an offence not to immobilise your vehicle before leaving it). Specific instructions were contained in a Ministry of War pamphlet, *The Immobilisation of Vehicles in the event of an Invasion*: if petrol driven, the distributor head and leads should be removed or, failing this, the carburettor. If diesel driven, the injection pump and connection were to be removed. In both cases the final instruction was to 'hide the parts removed well away from the vehicle'. If this was not done, Police would pull out the ignition leads and deflate the tyres. The idea was to prevent enemy agents from using them. The usual fine for non-observance was 10/-.

The blackout regulations for motorists were stringent, leading to many minor accidents. Apertures in side lamps could not exceed 2 inches in diameter, which in turn had to be covered by two thicknesses of newspaper. Tissue paper was insufficient. Lamp reflectors had to be blackened inside. The red glass of rear lamps also had to be covered with two thicknesses of newspaper. Headlights were required to be covered or painted completely except for a horizontal slit 2/3rd of an inch wide. The reflector had to be blackened and a shield fitted over the top of the lamp so that no direct ray of light was visible at eye level 25 yards in front of the car. During blackout hours, vehicles were restricted to a speed limit of 20 mph.

Cyclists had to take their bicycles off the road; it was not sufficient to prop them against the kerb or push them into an air-raid shelter. Cyclists were required to carry red rear lamps, hooded and

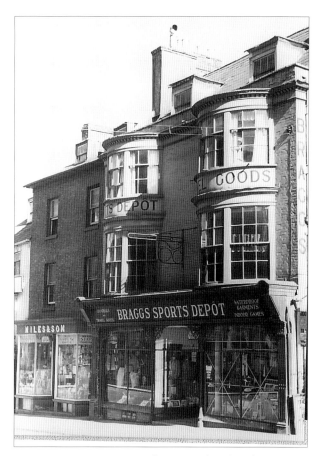

Braggs Sports Depot, South Street, showing the protective tape stuck to windows to reduce the damage from splintered glass.

dimmed so that no light was thrown directly upwards and no appreciable light was thrown on the ground, between sunset and sunrise. This was followed up by the *Echo* in the following day's edition when it was reported that Police Superintendent T.L. Carter quoted many cases where blackout requirement were not being adhered to. Examples given were skylights and panels over glass doors. The superintendent stressed that care must be taken when opening exterior doors, which on no occasion should be left open. To enforce this, police, both mobile and on foot, together with Air Raid Wardens would be patrolling the streets.

Generally, residents adapted well. Evening church services were held in the afternoon, whilst some motorists painted their mudguard and bumpers white. I remember seeing one car in South Street with a large white board at the back, supposedly so that vehicles travelling behind him could judge the distance between the two vehicles. From September 6 cars could no longer be parked without lights on Weymouth Avenue and South Walks Road. The Borough Council also helped by painting white some kerbs, lamp-posts, pillar box plinths and telegraph poles. From September 13 it became an offence to light a bonfire during the hours of darkness.

One Dorchester man received quite a shock when he was prosecuted for smoking in the street. To ironic shouts of 'put that cigarette out', common sense prevailed and it was decided that, provided one did not strike a succession of matches, all was well!

Some prosecutions did take place. The *Echo* reported that Mr John Galloway of the Antelope Hotel, Dorchester, had been fined £3 by the borough magistrates for permitting a light to be displayed during the blackout. Although a guest had left a curtain open, as proprietor he was deemed responsible. A day later a Mr Richard Tory was also fined £3 at the Dorchester Police Court for displaying an unauthorised light on a motor vehicle.

In November 1940 a poster campaign was carried out in Dorchester with such slogans as 'Where there is light, there is life' and 'Help beat Hitler by helping one another'. The opportunity was also taken to remind railway passengers that there were no lights on trains. Both the GWR and SR stations carried posters demanding 'Is your journey really necessary?'. Anyone who did travel by train found fares increasing all the time, late trains and overcrowding (nothing changes!). When a siren sounded, the train had to stop at the next station so that passengers, if they so wished, could leave the train and seek shelter. In due course the train slowly continued its journey, at 15 mph until November 1940 thereafter at 25 mph. With trains completely blacked out, several jokes surfaced: the only one I can risk committing to print was 'Girl in blacked-out train – 'Take your hand off my knee . . . no, not you!'

In December 1939 restrictions were slightly modified – 'diffused' lighting known as 'glimmer' or 'pin-prick' lighting was sanctioned. Minor concessions were also made to the lighting of shop windows. One household item, taken for granted before the war, suddenly became an essential part of daily life – the torch. But they soon became scarce, as did their batteries. Even torches, or rather their users, fell foul of the over-zealous Air Raid Wardens, and one often heard the shout of 'Keep that b....y torch pointing down and not up at the sky'.

Certainly the blackout caused much discomfort, perhaps best summed up by a cartoon that appeared in 1944. It showed a man jumping up and down in frustration and shouting 'When this foul blackout is finally over, I'm going to open every window and turn on every light and I'm going to go round to every house, ring their bells and shout 'Put that light on'. Most of us who lived through the blackout can surely identify with this? One popular song at the time was 'When the lights come on again, all over the world' sung by Penny Lee.

When the blackout did finally end many of Dorchester's 360 street lights didn't work – hardly surprising after years of disuse. When they were repaired it did mean, of course, that lovers had to find less public places to do their courting! Perhaps the only one good aspect of the blackout was that people appreciated the beauty of the night sky, although on moonlit evenings it was felt that German bomber crews would be better able to see their targets.

Schools

Perhaps because I attended school during the early war years, my memory is quite good on this subject – the so called 'best years of one's life'.

Dorchester Grammar School, Culliford Road. As early as 1938 senior pupils dug air raid trenches. They were situated under avenues of beech trees (many still there today), alongside the continuation of 'Chalky Lane' and on the path leading out to the Wareham Road. They were originally open, but as they quickly filled up with rainwater they were covered over with a combination of corrugated iron and flattened tar barrels. These were then covered over with soil and chalk. Duckboards were placed inside to walk on. The trenches were in constant use during the Battle of Britain and although we were supposed

to take our school books with us, I never remember any work being done as we were far more interested in what was happening in the sky above!

Classroom windows were painted over and criss-crossed with tape to help prevent injury from splintered glass should bombs drop. There were long blackout curtains in the Assembly Hall/Gymnasium.

Regular gas mask drill was carried out. In the early days of the war, teachers and prefects stood at the school gates to ensure all pupils were carrying their respirators. Many of the younger teachers left to serve in the armed forces.

The school had its own Officer Training Corps (OTC), later to become the Junior Training Corps (JTC). Although affiliated to the Dorsetshire Regiment, the Corps had its own distinctive cap badge. When I joined we were still being issued with First World War uniforms – service dress, puttees, and caps. We drilled with old 1900 Mauser rifles and others made from wood.

I can still remember the excitement when we handed in our old uniforms and were given

Dorchester Grammar School from the air, photographed shortly after the war. The avenues of beech trees are where trenches were dug to shelter from air raids. In the background, between the railway and Prince of Wales Road, can be seen some of the lines of concrete Dragons' Teeth intended to halt the German advance in the wake of an invasion.

battledress and soft forage caps. Eventually we were issued with .303 rifles and a real Bren gun. We took examinations at the barracks to achieve being awarded War Certificate A and Certificate B badges for wear on our uniforms.

The CO was Lt Whitaker assisted by 2nd Lt Newte and later by 2nd Lt Russell. Parade took place on Tuesday afternoons and the Corps also attended all the various parades that regularly took place in the town. While I was in the Corps, the Company Sergeant Major was Henry Tilling, Ralph Moore was Quartermaster Sergeant and my platoon commander was 'Jenny' Reynolds. In 1942 an Air Training Corps (ATC) was formed at the school with Maths master 'Saffy' Fox as the CO. Junior officers were Flavell and Brown and their Warrant Officer was 'Treacle' Treviss, ex

Royal Flying Corps.

Later in the war the school allowed pupils back into school during the normal summer holidays. These were great fun. We were read stories by volunteer masters, held sports and watched films. I particularly enjoyed a special game of 'touch' held in the school gymnasium. Mats were placed on the floor, the PT apparatus arranged around the gym, and all the ropes and ladders were lowered. Using them as a means of moving, together with the bars on two sides of the gym, we had to escape from our pursuer without touching the ground at any point. One 'spin off' was that it allowed pupils to meet the staff on an informal basis – quite unusual in those days. Some pupils worked on neighbouring farms and some did postal rounds at Christmas.

Life went on, but the horror of war was brought home to us when, at school assembly, the Headmaster 'Monty' Hill would read out the names of former pupils who had been killed in action.

The Dorset County School for Girls (The Green School). In September 1939 boys from Colliton Street Boys School joined about fifty volunteers to dig trenches for the girls of the Green School in Coburg Road.

When the air raid siren sounded all pupils had to remain where they were until Miss Ruegg, the Headmistress, appeared, complete with tin helmet on her head and several blasts from her whistle. Upon the whistle the girls had to stand up, whilst maintaining complete silence, pick up their gas masks and walk (on no account, run!) in line to the school tennis court, then run for the trenches (still in their lines!). A roll call of names was taken as they entered the trench. They then crouched or sat on the duck boards at the bottom of the trench until the all clear sounded.

The winter of 1940 was extremely cold, so much so that ink was known to freeze in the ink wells and bottles of water in the desk froze and exploded. However, the girls were still required to go to the trenches in balaclavas and warm clothes. The winter was also wet and the uncovered trench soon filled with water. It was then decided that the girls would remain in the school. Parts of the building, including under the staircases, were reinforced, and some girls recall sitting on library books until the all-clear sounded. One former pupil remembers the siren sounding during the sitting of the School Certificate French exam. Everyone had to promise they would not discuss the paper whilst they were in the trench. If the siren should sound either on their way to or on the way from school, there were certain 'safe' houses the girls could shelter in. Gas mask drills were held regularly.

The school had their own Girls Training Corps (GTC) and I well remember some of the NCO's – Margaret Screen, Mary Pidden, and Janet Wilkinson.

Maud Road School had a zig-zag blast wall built at the school. When the air-raid siren sounded, teachers and the school caretaker, often wearing tin hats, would direct the children to the school trenches. Often the teachers would sing nursery rhymes and the children would join in.

Icen Way School used Wollaston Field when the air raid siren sounded. Their trenches were just inside the wall in Icen Way, now occupied by the Social Services. The trenches were open and despite having duckboards were usually partly filled by rainwater, meaning that children had to stand until the all-clear sounded. As they were instructed to keep their heads below the top of the trenches, 'so that you cannot be seen from the air', the taller ones had to crouch!

The Modern School had blast walls built in the school corridors and the pupils were required to shelter under the stairs when the siren sounded.

Colliton Street Boys School (known to its pupils as Colliton College!). Pupils helped dig open trenches for both the Green School and Maud Road School. They themselves used trenches in the grounds of Colliton Park, which had lattice duckboards and camouflage netting over the top (the netting was made by the pupils). They also painted over all white walls with camouflage colours. They later used the basement of County Hall.

St Georges Infants School, Fordington. At the beginning of the war, children from the school, hearing the siren, walked to the mill in Mill Street to take shelter under the mill wheel housing. Later trenches were dug in an arc in front of Victoria

Terrance, in Salisbury Field, and the children then used these.

West Fordington Infants School, School Lane. Slit trenches were dug by the school on the right hand side. Incidentally this area was once the Dorchester Regiment cemetery, and two existing houses still have regimental badges in the brickwork.

School Milk

During the war, each child was given a small bottle of milk to drink during morning school. These were the days of glass bottles with a cardboard disc in the top of each bottle. The disc also contained a small hole through which a drinking straw could be inserted. Wonderful in theory, but invariably when pressing one's thumb down to make the opening, you pushed too hard and the milk spurt up into your face. Happy memories!

Children were also expected to take cod liver oil either in liquid form or a capsule. And most of us had to suffer a weekly intake (usually Saturday night) of a spoonful of syrup of figs – a horrible taste – 'to keep ones bowels open'. Not such happy memories!

Identity Cards

Following a National Registration Census on 29 September 1939, identity cards were issued carrying one's name, address and National Registration Number. These cards were required to be shown on request at any time but despite Dorchester being within a restricted defence area, I was never asked to produce mine (and yes, I do still have my original card!). The original thinking for the issue of these cards was that it would identify the holder so that they would not be mistaken for either a deserter from the armed forces or a fifth column enemy agent. Rather laughable really, as any real enemy agent would have obtained a forged card long before he started spying!

Members of local rambling clubs, as well as having to carry their identity cards also had to carry their membership cards. This was entirely understandable as anyone 'wandering around' immediately made others suspicious and Dorchester was, at the time, rife with enemy agent

rumours. Some carried bracelets with name and identity card number, similar to the 'dog tags' carried by all British military forces.

Passports

On the 4th September 1939 it was announced that the validity of all endorsements on existing British passports had been cancelled. Further endorsements would now be required. No one could leave the country without an exit permit from the Passport and Permit Office and permission from the immigration officer at the port of departure.

Photography

In the *Echo* of September 12 1939 it was stated that the War Office had announced severe restrictions on the use of photography, giving a long list of items that it was forbidden to photograph (far too long to list here). The announcement went on to say that by taking a photograph it placed suspicion on the taker, and their advice was simply that it was best not to take any photographs at all. Photographs of anything that could possibly be of use to the enemy could lead to prosecution and imprisonment. This perhaps is the main reason why there are so few photographs of wartime Dorchester, together with the fact that cameras were expensive. Most families made do with perhaps one small box Brownie. Film was almost unobtainable, all supplies going to the armed forces. The only place you could get a film, and then in rolls of 6 only, unless you were lucky enough to get a Kodak which had 8 in a roll, was at Curiosity Corner (in Bryer Ash Coal shop in Trinity Street) run by local photographer Evan Jones.

Food Rationing

Although food rationing was first discussed in 1935 it is perhaps surprising that it was not immediately introduced on the declaration of war. The reason was that the government did not want to cause panic.

In 1938, my father who worked for the High West Street solicitors, Lock Reed & Lock, was seconded by Major H.O. Lock to work for the Ministry of Food and be responsible for the

preparation and eventual issue of ration books for the Dorchester area. Offices were set up in a small room in Grey School Passage by Holy Trinity Church, later moving to premises now occupied by Herrings in High West Street. Other moves followed and their office was eventually established at Savernake House at the Top O'Town. Most of the staff were recruited from wives of soldiers stationed in the town.

Once war broke out we were told that Britain's food cupboards were full and could keep the the country well fed for several months. Strangely enough the demand for rationing came from the general public. Even before food rationing was officially introduced, Dorchester shopkeepers introduced their own unofficial rationing. Food rationing was officially initiated in January 1940. Ration books were issued with green coupons for meat, yellow for butter and margarine and orange for cooking fats. The system of tendering a coupon for an item of food was both simple and effective, but having to register with one retailer only caused a lot of resentment.

Butter, sugar, bacon and ham were the first items to be weekly rationed – 4oz of bacon or ham, 12ozs sugar (reduced in 1942 to 8ozs) and 4ozs

The second building on the left was Savernake House, High West Street, the wartime headquarters of the Ministry of Food, from where all ration books were issued.

butter. Meat went on ration in March – 1/10d per week (later reduced to 1/2d of which 2d was for corned beef) for everyone over the age of 6, 11d for smaller children. Tea rationing followed in July – 2ozs and we were advised 'one spoonful for each person and none for the pot'. Also in July the National Milk scheme provided a pint of milk a day at the reduced price of 2d, and free for every expectant or nursing mother and every child under five not attending school.

In March 1941 jam, marmalade and syrup required coupons, followed by mincemeat, lemon curd and honey (from 8ozs to 2lbs according to season). In May the cheese ration was 1oz per week, later increased to 2ozs.

In 1942, eggs were supplemented by 'Dried Eggs', quickly followed by 'Dried Milk'. In the same year sweets and chocolate were rationed with the coupon being called 'personal points' – 8ozs every four weeks. Dark chocolate replaced milk chocolate, the silver paper was replaced by waxed paper and a 'ration chocolate' selling at 2½d a bar, was introduced by Cadburys. I remember a bar of Nestlé's chocolate with 'Milk' deleted on the wrapper and replaced by 'Plain'.

Mid war, a week's ration was 2ozs tea, 8ozs sugar, 4ozs jam, 3ozs sweets, 2ozs lard, 2ozs butter, 2ozs margarine, 4ozs cheese, 4ozs bacon, ¾ lb of meat, and one egg.

Food was scarce and the need for nutrition and a balanced diet was impressed on the nation. Housewives received advice from many sources. After the 8 a.m. news the BBC ran a five minute 'Kitchen Front'. Food facts appeared in the newspapers and on screens at both the Plaza and Palace cinemas. A leaflet called *The Kitchen Front* became popular at a cost of 6d a copy: it contained 122 wartime recipes including pea pod soup, jugged kippers, black pudding hot pot, bacon and haricot bean hash, cooked lettuce and uncooked cauliflower salad, and many more mouth watering dishes! Amongst the puddings were Marmalade Pudding and Wartime Queen of Puddings.

We ate 'Woolton Pie' and one of the few meats excluded from rationing, SPAM (SPiced HAM). Potatoes were 'plugged' at every opportunity and 'Potato Pete' became a well known cartoon character: he was drawn as a large potato wearing a trilby hat, gaiters and boots, a piece of straw in his mouth, and with a garden fork over his shoulder. One of his gimmicks was to adapt a nursery rhyme – 'Little Jack Horner sat in a corner eating potato pie. He took a large bite and said with delight "Oh what a strong boy am I"'.

We were also urged to eat loads of carrots, helped by another cartoon character – Doctor Carrot. Books included *101 Creative uses for a Carrot*! Although the diet was somewhat boring, no one ever went hungry. Although onions disappeared – no supplies from France or the Channel Islands – eggs and vegetables were sold by local farmers at Dorchester market and from barrows on Cornhill (many vegetables were also grown in back gardens and allotments) and fish (never rationed) was obtainable from local fishmongers. Rabbits, hares, pheasants, partridge and wood pigeon were also freely available. In fact the nation had never been as healthy as it was during the war years!

As well as Dorchester market, vegetables not rationed were sold by local farmers from barrows in Cornhill.

Animals and Birds

The day after the war broke out it was announced that nearly 7000 dogs and 5000 cats had been painlessly destroyed in London a few days earlier, but owners were urged to think twice before putting their pets down. There was plenty of animal food in the country and as an alternative, urban owners of pets were to consider sending them to the country. If this proved impossible, you were instructed not to take dogs with you when going shopping, as they were not allowed in public air raid shelters. Dog owners were also advised to exercise them locally so as to be able to quickly return home if the siren sounded. When taking your dog into your own air raid shelter, you were advised to place cotton wool in its ears, as well as a lead and muzzle to restrain it if it became hysterical during an air raid. Another suggestion was to obtain bromide from the chemist to give to the dog before a raid! There were gas masks for dogs. Cat owners were told to forget about them as 'cats can take care of themselves far better than we can'.

Even birds did not escape the war. *The Dorset Echo* of September 5 announced that anyone keeping racing or homing pigeons should immediately report to the police. Heavy penalties might be imposed on anyone keeping these birds without a police permit.

THREE

The Phoney War
September 1939 – April 1940

When war against Germany was declared no one quite knew what to expect. So far we had grown used to gas masks, shortages, rationing, the blackout, and queues which grew steadily longer (and slower). With our armed forces helping France, Dorchester had received its quota of evacuees from London, and was now preparing for the battle on the Home Front. The town next turned to the task of preparing itself for the expected air raids against a background of the coldest January and February in Dorchester for 45 years.

AIR RAID SIRENS

Tests carried out during 1939 showed that the original air raid siren in Maumbury Ring, erected in March 1940, was quite inadequate to serve the whole town, especially if the wind was in the wrong direction! Tests were then carried out with sirens mounted on trailers but these proved unsuccessful.

A report of May 1940 stated that 'In view of the inadequacies of the existing siren, approval has been given for the erection of additional sirens in Dorchester'. Instructions were given that each siren be fixed to the roof of a building or raised 20 feet above the ground on scaffold poles or steel towers. Over each siren was to be a baffle board to distribute the sound.

The chosen locations for Dorchester's three sirens were:

The Barracks, Top O'Town. The siren was placed on the centre of the front of the Keep, not visible from the road. After the war it was removed for renovation, which proved to be too expensive and it was never replaced.

Maumbury Rings. The siren was located roughly two thirds along the ridge inside Weymouth Avenue towards the Maumbury Road railway bridge. Well remembered by an electrician who, when working for a local radio shop, plugged into it for his amplifiers when they were required for announcements at public events!

Daubennys Farm, Fordington. Again, raised on scaffolding in the farmyard next to and reaching higher than the churchyard of Fordington St George church. Alas, neither the farm nor the yard are still there having been sold and replaced by housing.

Warnings of the approach of enemy aircraft would be issued by RAF Fighter Command to the Group concerned via the Post Office, who would pass the warning to the Chief Constable of Dorset who was responsible for the siting of and operation of Air Raid Warning sirens, set off by remote control from Dorchester Police Station in Weymouth Avenue, installed by the Post Office.

We were advised that in the event of threatened air raids, warnings would be given by sirens and/or hooters (in Dorchester it was sirens), emitting a warbling note changing every few seconds. Who will ever forget that wailing sound? On hearing the warning we were ordered to 'Take shelter' and to stay there until we heard the 'Raiders passed' signal which would be given by continuously sounding the siren for two minutes on the same note (also unforgettable).

Residents living in the Queen's Avenue, Maiden Castle Road and Victoria Park areas often heard the Weymouth sirens before they heard the Dorchester ones.

On March 1 1940 it was decided to test Dorchester's air raid sirens on the first Monday of each month at 2 p.m. until further notice. One small child in Dorchester asked by her parents why she could not get to sleep replied, 'I can't go to sleep yet, the siren hasn't sounded'.

In Dorchester the first 'yellow warning' was received on June 17 1940 and four days later the first siren sounded (apart from when sounded for practice testing purposes).

When Germany resorted to night attacks against the cities of England, night after night the Dorchester siren would sound at around 8 p.m. and we heard German bombers overhead, usually on their way to Bristol, Coventry or Exeter: Dorchester seemed to be on their direct flight path. The all clear usually sounded between 7-8 a.m. the following morning. No one who lived through those nights will ever forget the distinctive, uneven, throb of those German aircraft, described by someone as a deep voice repeating over and over, 'Where are you? Where are you?'

As far as Dorchester was concerned the sirens caused far greater disruption and disturbance than the few bombs that were dropped on the town. Quite apart from the apprehension and fear of if, when and where bombs might fall, there was the inconvenience of having to abandon whatever one was doing and making for some form of air raid shelter. Everything was affected – even opening hours.

A popular war-time song was 'When they sound the last 'all clear'. The discontinuance of the Air Raid Warning Siren came into effect on the 4 June 1945 but Dorchester retained theirs to be used to call out National Fire Service personnel in order to combat fires.

AIR RAID SHELTERS

CELLARS, BASEMENTS, AND VAULTS

When the ARP services were mobilised it was decreed that trenches were to be dug to take cover in and that cellars and basements of both public and private buildings were to be requisitioned for use as public air raid shelters. It was estimated that these would provide shelter for the 10-15% of the local population likely to be out in the streets when the air raid siren sounded.

On the left is The Three Mariners in High East Street, under which was the most popular air raid shelter in the town. It was entered under the arch and a side door which led down steps into the shelter.

Perhaps the one that is best remembered by Dorchester folk is the cellar under the Three Mariners public house in High East Street. When Goulds was also in High East Street, on the corner with Icen Way, they even advised their customers in a reassuring advertisement that stated 'There is a public air raid shelter opposite our premises in High East Street'. Sadly now demolished, there is no doubt this was the most popular shelter in the town and many are the stories of temporary occupants, on hearing the siren, 'stocking up' from the bar before going below and sleeping right through the all clear!

High West Street provided another air raid shelter in cellars under what was the Dorset County Club. The main entrance was between the club and Lloyds Bank as it then was, and it still exists albeit in a modified form. Another entrance may have been from the pavement outside the club. The stone slab seats are still there as are two air vents and a notice indicating the emergency exit into the next building, the Dorset County Library. In the same painted style of lettering there is still another notice pointing to the light

This photograph of the Mayor's Parade in 1943 passing St Peter's Church, in which American officers took part, is of interest in that it shows the direction sign on the church railings pointing to the air raid shelter in the cellars of the Dorset County Club in High West Street.

switch. The shelter was identified by a sign fastened to the railings above the wall of St Peter's church. On a black sign in white paint were a large letter 'S' (for shelter), a direction arrow and the words 'Shelter for 100' and '35 yards'. The measurements are exact – I have measured them! The emergency exit is now blocked up. The cellars under the old library are still there but were used only as an exit and not as a shelter.

The top of High West Street also had cellars for the public. These were under the Wessex Tea Rooms (now the Wessex Royale Hotel) although the entrance was from Princes Street. There were steps behind what is now the health food shop 'Down to Earth' – still there as is the front of the shelter, now used as a store. The entrance to the remaining cellar is now blocked, but during the war the tunnels ran right through the health shop, the next door premises (now a carpet shop) and under the Tea Rooms (later used as a rifle range). The tunnels under what is now the carpet shop once had benches along the walls.

Trinity Street was well provided with these basement and cellar public shelters. In 1939 number 27 was Harry Golday's Bluebird Café, while numbers 28 to 30 were private houses. All had large cellars and were required by emergency laws to link them – 'linked basements and pavement vaults to be used as Public Air Raid shelters – coal shutes can be used as entrances'. In this instance there were proper entrances. Steps still lead down from inside the buildings that were 28 to 30, but the main public entrance was via the passageway leading from Trinity Street to Alexander Terrace. One went through a door in the wall and then down stone steps to the shelter. The cellars were reinforced, benches installed and signs pointing to the emergency exit – this can still be seen, situated at No 28 (now an estate agent) as a black grill almost two feet up the base of the building from the pavement. A large direction sign to this shelter was affixed to the wall above W.H. Smith & Son in South Street with a large 'S' and 'Shelter for 220 in Trinity St', and an arrow pointing up the passageway between what is now The National Westminster Bank and Marks & Spencers.

Further along the street was another large public air raid shelter built to accommodate 100 people under Genge and Co, stretching from Princes Street to High West Street. Although the cellars are still there, the entrance, at the rear of the premises with stone steps leading down, has long been demolished.

At the other end of Trinity Street in the triangular junction with South Street were public lavatories – the men's entrance from South Street – the women's from Trinity Street. Although never listed as a public air raid shelter, they were used as such when the sirens sounded.

There was also an air raid shelter cellar under the malthouse in Charles Street, now long since demolished.

Another cellar/vault that was used by many Dorchester residents as an air raid shelter was the space under the bandstand in the Borough Gardens, which is remembered by many as always smelling damp. In November 1939 it was decided that air raid shelters were to be provided for staff of the Dorset County Council offices At the same time, trenches were to be dug in the gardens of Holly Bank, and at Wadham House – at a minimum cost!

The basements of County Hall in Colliton Park were used – not only by staff but members of the public, especially those who lived at the top of the Grove. Similar shelters were provided in the basements of New Shire Hall.

Residents living in the Fordington area used the cellars under the Old Mill in Mill Street. Entry was through the mill gates, into where there was a long room where mattresses were placed along the floor for people to sit and sleep on. There was a table in the centre.

It has been suggested that before the men's lavatories at the back of the Corn Exchange in North Square were officially opened, and even afterwards, they were used as a public air raid shelter. I am unable to confirm this. I certainly remember them as the smelliest public toilets I have ever had the misfortune to use – and only then if desperate! – and like many others were delighted to see them demolished.

PURPOSE-BUILT OR ADAPTED SHELTERS

As early as the beginning of 1940, Dorchester councillors were pressing for purpose-built surface air raid shelters and in June, H.S. Matthews, the County Architect, submitted a drawing for the proposed shelters.

Sanction had been given for the provision of shelters on the basis of 3% of the borough's population. Each was to be constructed of reinforced brick, with a reinforced concrete floor and roof, normally in two long compartments, side

W.H. Smith & Son, South Street. Above the shop is a large direction sign to the air raid for 220 people in Trinity Street.

by side, each to accommodate 32 persons and measuring 23' 3" x 16' 6" with 6' 6" internal headroom. By July 24 it was reported that there were sufficent shelters for 830 people.

The purpose built/adapted air raid shelters were situated at:

Bowling Alley Walks. On the grass at the rear of the Junction Hotel car park buildings.

South Walks. Past the war memorial and the old James Foot premises, outside South Lodge (later a doctor's surgery and now a private residence), on

The damp cellar beneath the bandstand in the Borough Gardens was often used as an air raid shelter.

39

Just visible in the background is the purpose-built air raid shelter in South Walks between South Street and Charles Street. The site is now a small Garden of Remembrance.

the present Garden of Remembrance. For a while after the war, the shelter was used to store equipment and material required to maintain the Walks.

Yard next to the old Fire Station, Trinity Street. Roughly where the present public toilets are situated.

Top O'Town Car Park. Again, roughly where the present public toilets are.

Greyhound Yard. From South Street, there was a passageway known as Greyhound Passage, then a row of cottages, when it opened up into a small shopping area (Sid Lear's butchers shop was one of them) and into Greyhound Yard (now covered by Waitrose). This later became a public car park and the shelter was built on the corner.

Salisbury Fields. From Icen Way, opposite the three modern statues of the Martyrs by Dame Elisabeth Frink, there is a path into Salisbury Fields, as there also is from South Walks Road, entered by stone steps. Where these two paths meet, they divide, the main one continuing down past the old gasworks to London Road, the other, a smaller one, curving round and cutting across Salisbury Fields towards High Street, Fordington. As soon as this path begins to curve, there is a strip of grass going up to the garden walls of the houses along South Walks Road. Before the three small and two larger trees, a public air raid shelter was erected, almost up to the garden walls.

The Fairfield. When one came out from the old entrance next to the Southern Railway station and crossed over into Fairfield Road, leading from Maumbury Road, an air raid shelter was built just inside the iron railings, a few yards from the entrance to Fairfield Road.

The Cemetery, Weymouth Avenue. Still in existence is a smaller than usual air raid shelter in the cemetery grounds. Visible from Weymouth Avenue, it is well built with nearly solid walls and concrete roof. With just the one entrance/exit there are marks where seats were fixed to the walls. Certainly used by the staff and possibly by people using the cemetery.

Prince of Wales Road. A 1957 map of the old Dorchester Southern Railway buildings and track shows an air raid shelter located in what is now the garden of number 84 – these are the old SR cottages. The shelter was on high ground where the brick wall curves round from the extension from Monmouth Road railway bridge to meet Prince of Wales Road. Entrance to the shelter up the steep steps of number 84. The present occupier remembers it was still there when she moved in, partly above and partly below ground. Still remaining is an air vent rising some 2' above the ground, albeit filled with soil.

Prince's Street. Just outside the kitchens of the Dorset County Hospital was a large air raid shelter, primarily for the use of staff and patients. It survived until the late 1960s

Noah's Ark Public House. Outside this public house was a stone construction with rounded top, resembling a bee-hive. The original use of this structure is not known but it was certainly used by the general public as an air-raid schelter.

Purpose built public surface air raid shelters had no recovery value and most were demolished soon after the war, either as hardcore by local authorities in their post-war housing schemes or sold off to private builders. Dorchester's shelters lasted longer than most other local towns.

Trenches were quickly filled in and disappeared from view under local authority arrangements.

PRIVATE AIR RAID SHELTERS
Once war was declared we were advised to dig our own air raid shelters in the garden by way of a trench and to ensure it was covered with a

40

minimum of 18 inches of earth. In Dorchester, it was decided Anderson shelters would be provided for out of doors and Morrison shelters for indoors. The Morrison shelter was a large steel framework 6' x 4" and 2' 9" high with a steel mattress and wire mesh sides to accommodate two adults and two children lying down: they were free to lower income families and £7 to others. Many families used theirs as a table. If the siren sounded during a meal, it was not unknown for some to dive into the shelter whilst others continued with their meal. It provided protection against the effect of blast and splinters though not from a direct hit by a high explosive bomb.

The Anderson shelter was to be erected in a hole 7' 6" x 6' to a depth of 4'. Designed to hold six people and built to withstand a 500lb bomb, the top was covered over with corrugated iron and garden soil. Like the Morrison they were free to lower income earners and £7 to others. They were stored in a building in Colliton Park, the two large doors of which were in Glyde Path Road on the left hand side going down the hill towards Hangman's Cottage.

Users of these shelters were advised to ensure there were always adequate supplies of first aid items, snacks, hot drinks in a vacuum flask, cold water, rugs and flash lamps. Suggestions of items to also take with them included a pack of playing cards and 'something decent to read'.

To those without either shelter – and that was the majority of Dorchester residents – the most popular place to shelter was under the stairs or under a heavy table. Official advice was 'on no account look out of the windows' during an air raid. My father always obeyed all the instructions and, as soon as the air raid siren had sounded, sought refuge in a downstairs room. My mother and I, on the other hand, immediately rushed out into the back garden 'to see what was happening'!

A report of May 1945 confirmed that all the shelters had been closed, but that their demolition or removal was considered unjustified in view of the need of labour for more pressing needs, e.g. provision of housing. Should anyone want to retain their shelter they were entitled to buy them for a fixed price of £1 for Andersons and £1 10/- for Morrisons.

The only surviving above ground air raid shelter in Dorchester is the small brick and concrete shelter near the entrance to the Cemetery in Weymouth Avenue.

The sounding of the air raid sirens and the subsequent journey to the shelters did spawn one war-time garment . . . 'the siren suit' – a one-piece outfit made popular by Winston Churchill one could slip into easily and quickly. It became the standard dress for the air raid shelter.

Although there was much hectic activity preparing for the expected air raids, the anticipated attacks did not materialise and life went on pretty much as before. This period later became known as 'The Phoney War' and some, with longer memories than others, referred to it as 'The Bore War', a pun on the Boer War!

Well known firms exploited the war to publicise their product – Puritan Soap offered 'Double Ration Lather', Bemax placed their cereals in tins to make it gas proof, and Frys offered their chocolate spread as 'solving the butter problem'. Even the cardboard milk bottle tops had slogans such as 'Raw materials are War materials' and 'Milk for Vigour and Victory'.

This was a time when people were optimistic about the short time it would take to beat Germany. We sang songs like 'We'll hang out the washing on the Siegfried Line . . . if the Siegfried Line's still there'! There was also a rather crude verse relating to the anatomy of the German hierarchy, and I remember seeing posters around Dorchester that bore a picture of Hitler and the words 'Wanted for Murder'.

FOUR

Dunkirk

The 'Phoney War' came to a dramatic end with the defeat of the French and the evacuation of the remains of the British Expeditionary Force from the French coastline, centred on the small port of Dunkirk.

Our troops, together with those of our allies, started to land at Weymouth on 26th May 1940 where they boarded trains for reception centres and army camps all over the country. Living as I did alongside the Southern Railway I well remember watching endless trains going past filled with shattered, exhausted and injured troops. As they passed slowly though Dorchester Southern Railway station local residents passed them cigarettes, drinks and food. Some soldiers managed a V sign but most were just too weary. I feel sure it was the same for those that passed through the Great Western Railway station.

Although concern had been expressed that as Dorchester was already full of military personnel there would be no room for a further influx, many public and private buildings were commandeered to house the remnants of the BEF, among them the Corn Exchange, Plume of Feathers skittle alley, Trinity Institute, WI Hall, All Saints Hall, The Moule Institute and church halls – as well as many private houses. Many were billeted in the Pheonix yard – well supplied with bread and fresh buns from Virgins the bakers next door.

Even now, more than sixty-five years later, I can recall watching the trains arriving at the Southern Railway station – these were the days when they had to travel up to Culliford Road Bridge and then reverse into the station – and being shocked at the state of many of the soldiers. Some wore only one boot, many had no boots at all. Uniforms were torn, dirty and partly missing. The wounded were bandaged, some were bloodstained, others had their arms in a sling. But perhaps the lasting memory was the shell-shocked look on their faces.

We still talk about 'Dunkirk spirit' and for me it was captured in the scene at the station. Ignoring the buses that were waiting to take them to the barracks for assembly and billeting out, they formed three lines and marched along Fairfield Road, into Cornwall Road and to the Keep. Perhaps 'marching' is not quite the correct word – walked and stumbled would be a better description, some with sticks, some with home-made crutches, some being helped along by their comrades. But what a sight! And many that lined the streets, cried openly – a beaten army, yes but still with their heads held high, still proud. It made one so proud to be British! Unforgettable. It was later reported that once they had assembled and reported in, they sat down to their first good meal for days, but so many were so tired they simply fell asleep over the meal.

Strange how one remembers small things at a time like that – one man was carrying a Belgian hare – a mascot perhaps?

Members of the 2nd Battalion The Dorsetshire Regiment were evacuated from Dunkirk on May 30th. Most landed at Margate but some came ashore at Weymouth and made the short trip to their headquarters in Dorchester.

The town suddenly seemed packed with soldiers, some simply wandering about, others asleep on the pavements. I remember High West Street in particular with dishevelled troops sitting on the pavement kerbstones: to cross the road one had to step over them. The Borough Gardens and all the Walks were packed with sleeping troops and one young lady returning from her boarding school for the holidays was astonished to see her parents' garden full of soldiers, all of them fast asleep.

The residents of Dorchester were equal to the occasion and invited them into their homes, fed them, offered them cigarettes and helped them get in touch with their families and friends. Most needed a good hot bath. One family provided baths for up to thirty soldiers a day; there was no time to wash the towels, they were dried on the boiler and made ready for the next one!

The last troops were evacuated on the 4 June, but during their stay there was a fair in the Fairfield and servicemen were allowed free rides on the 'Dodgems'.

Lloyds Bank offered to encash French francs so that French servicemen who had escaped could buy postcards to send to their families in France.

Dorchester Cricket Club played a team from the Durham Light Infantry after their return from Dunkirk – won by the D.L.I. who scored 204 for 7 wickets and then bowled Dorchester out for 193.

To give thanks for the miracle of Dunkirk, a National Day of Prayer was held throughout the county and in Dorchester there were services in all the churches, soldiers marching down from the barracks and being dropped off en route. Each soldier left his rifle outside the church with a guard at each church.

I attended St Peter's church where the Rev Markby conducted the service. A very moving occasion with the inevitable sounding of the Air Raid siren and the arrival of German aircraft over Dorchester, the A.A. gunfire, the sound of aircraft machine guns and the dropping of a few bombs which, thankfully, caused no loss of life.

Many friendships were formed whilst these troops were here, some lasting for many years.

FIVE

Invasion Threatens

Although the evacuation of the remains of the British Expeditionery Force was hailed as a miracle – and indeed it was, the nation was brought down to earth on 4 June 1940 when the new Prime Minister, Winston Churchill, addressing the House of Commons, pointed out that wars were not won by evacuation and Dunkirk represented a colossal military disaster. He went on to talk about the dangers of invasion.

Several 'If the Invader Comes' public information leaflets were soon issued. Their basic message was that nothing should be given to any German. 'Do not tell him anything. Hide your food and your bicycles, hide your maps and always think of your country before you think of yourself'. After Dunkirk, Great Britain stood alone against the German might – flushed with success and far better equipped.

Dorchester, like similar towns along the south coast of England, suddenly went into overdrive. Invasion committees were set up to prepare defences against the expected imminent invasion. If not quite panic, there was certainly a sense of urgency. Holes were dug in roads and bridges, which were then filled with concrete stoppers or plugs with handles allowing traffic to pass over them. In the event of enemy vehicles approaching, the plugs would be replaced with iron rods. Bridges were often protected by concrete pillboxes intended to stem the German advance. Guns and even old tanks were dug in, anti-tank ditches were dug, anti-tank mines prepared for roads and bridges, and everywhere coils of barbed wire festooned streets and country lanes.

The design of the 12 official (there were many local variations) pillboxes differed considerably, but generally they were concrete bunkers fitted with openings through which our troops could fire at the enemy with rifles, Bren guns and anti-tank rifles. The Home Guard was also employed, their main weapon being the homemade 'Molotov cocktail'. The pillboxes were sited to protect specific targets, often in conjunction with anti-tank obstacles such as concrete blocks and ditches. In the early days all sorts of objects were placed across roads: including old farm waggons and tree trunks. Gradually these were replaced with 500lbs cylindrical blocks of concrete, often with handles to enable them to be hauled into the roads. Later, permanent concrete blocks, commonly known as 'dragons teeth' were used. There were five basic designs – cubes, blocks (known as coffins), pyramids (known as pimples), cylinders and buoys.

Each design had its advantages and disadvantages, so whenever possible a mixture of all types were used. Their main purpose was to slow advancing tanks, thus creating an opportunity to destroy them with anti-tank guns. Five feet long lengths of steel scaffolding were also used, which were driven into the ground leaving them half exposed. Three feet high stacks of railway sleepers or timber poles were fixed by stakes in the ground.

A decision was made that should the Germans breach the sea and beach defences, our forces would fall back (the word retreat was never used) to 'Stop-Lines'. These were basically the next line of defence and created to prevent mobile columns bursting through the country as they had done so successfully in France.

Dorset and Hampshire were considered to be vulnerable to invasion and in July 1940 a special group, V Corps, was set up with its headquarters at Tidworth to defend the area. Dorchester was chosen to be part of a 'stop-line', and in August the town's 'stop-line' was provided with two-way anti-tank ditches to meet armoured advance from either direction, bridge demolitions were set in place and tank blocks established at important crossings. Pillboxes were built and concrete emplacements made for 6 pounder anti-tank guns. By the 25 August all work had been completed and in September further sites were designated for Dorchester. 52 pillboxes and 3 miles of anti-tank ditches were scheduled.

Ironically much of this new work took place after Hitler had shelved plans for an invasion and by June 1941 no further defence work was carried out.

DRAGONS TEETH IN DORCHESTER.

The urgency to complete these defences was reflected in the speed of construction. By November 1940 no fewer than 267 pipes, 10 irons and 137 cubes were in place – a total of 414 items at 34 separate locations.

By and large they followed the Great Western Railway and Southern Railway track and the River Frome, forming a triangle of defence around Dorchester which became 'a tank island'. In the order they were officially listed they were situated as follows:

1. Friary Hill: 7 pipes and 1 iron in a double line at the bottom of the hill.
2. Friary Cottage: 7 pipes across the road in a single line outside the cottage and just in front of the river.
3. Frome Terrace: 1 cube in the alleyway leading up to North Square, between numbers 19 and 20 Frome Terrace – just inside, from the road.
4. Orchard Street: 3 cubes in a single line at the eastern end of the street.
5. Glyde Path Road: 9 pipes in a double line at the bottom of the hill just before the road curves round into Northernhay.
6. Riverbank by Hangmans Cottage: 2 cubes by the side of the cottage on the banks of the stream that goes out to Blue Bridge.
7. Northernhay: 5 pipes in a double line, by Hangmans Cottage, just in Northernhay
8. Footpath, Hangmans Cottage to Glyde Path Road – 1 cube.
9. The Grove: 11 pipes, I iron and 1 cube in a double line at the bottom of the Grove opposite The Compasses Inn.
10. Millers Close: 6 pipes in a double line not far in

Prince of Wales Road. Three of the surviving line of dragons teeth on the railway bank between Southern Railway Cottages and Culliford Road bridge. This photograph was taken in 2001, before the hedging had grown up.

from The Grove.
11. School Lane: 1 cube at the Millers Close end of the lane.
12. Poundbury Road: 10 pipes, 1 iron and 5 cubes in a double line beside and across the railway bridge.
13. Marabout Barracks: 7 pipes in double lines at the West Gate, 4 pipes in double lines at the North Gate, 7 pipes in double lines at the Lower West Gate.
14. Bridport Road: 13 pipes in a double lines and 4 cubes near St Thomas' Road and by the Top O'Town car park.
15. The ones by the railway bridge were on both the banks, 2 opposite The Sydney Arms along St Thomas' Road and 2 across the road on the other side of Bridport Road. These are still in situ and although covered by brambles, grass and foliage are still visible from the road – certainly the largest dragons teeth I have ever seen.
16. Damers Road: 11 pipes and 2 cubes in a double line on the allotments, below the old workhouse and by the railway bridge. These were demolished when the new road leading up to the hospital from Damers Road to Bridport Road was built.
17. Great Western Railway Station: 13 pipes and 13 cubes in a double line at the approach to the station.
18. Weymouth Avenue and Maumbury Junction: 17 pipes, 1 iron and 19 cubes in a double line semi circle (partly on private land). Some in Maumbury Rings.
19. Maumbury Road: 13 pipes, 1 iron and 1 cube in double lines, 7 pipes and 1 cube in a double line on the railway bridge at the junction with Monmouth Road. Also on the bridge were 2 poles, one by Maumbury Rings, the other by the terrace of houses. On the pole by Maumbury Rings was hung a high circle of barbed wire, covered with sacking – presumably it was the

Napper's Mite, South Street. Just visible on the right is one of the concrete blocks which would have been used to block the entrance to New Street.

intention to uncut the wire and stretch it to the other pole to impede enemy troops. It stayed there long after war ended

20. Culliford Road: 5 pipes and 13 cubes (pyramid types) in a single line at the Southern Railway bridge (from the bridge to the entrance to the railway and partly on private property), 12 pipes in a double line, at the end of the bridge on the Prince of Wales' Road side.

21. Prince of Wales' Road: 14 cubes in a single line on the railway bank from the Southern Railway Cottages towards Culliford Road bridge. Although partly covered by shrubs, 9 are still visible from the road, all well preserved, and are a mixture of the rounded top, flat top and pyramid varieties of dragons teeth. These were then joined by a further 13 cubes that extended the line almost up to the gate leading into the railway siding.

22. Monmouth Road: 7 pipes in a double line under Monmouth Road railway bridge. The natural railway embankment defence was strengthened by the pegging of railway sleepers along its length and sites located for the laying of mines.

23. Prince of Wales' Road: 32 square cubes with rounded top in a single line from Monmouth Road railway bridge and along, just inside the allotments that ran along Prince of Wales' Road to the stone wall that was the boundary of the Dorset War Agriculture Executive Committee building (originally intended as a military hospital). All but two were demolished when the allotments and fields made way for the buildings that now occupy the site. These last 2, large and clad with corrugated iron, were right next to Monmouth Road railway bridge and were so covered by the hedge that they were only discovered quite recently when a digger dug out the hedge at the corner of the site. Now demolished.

24. Prince of Wales' Road: 10 pipes and 3 cubes in a double line at Rainborrow (private property).

25. Athelstan Road: 12 pipes, 1 iron and 1 cube in a double line across the road at the junction with King's Road.

26. King's Road: 22 pipes, 1 iron and 1 cube in a double line across the road from the junction with High Street Fordington and Little Britain. Before the permanent dragons teeth was concreted in, there was a mobile one with handles at the top for moving.

27. Alington Road: 13 pipes, 2 irons and 2 cubes in a double line just beyond where the road meets St Georges Road.

28. Holloway Road: 6 pipes, 1 iron in a double line. Just beyond the river bridge by the Old Mill.

29. Swan Bridge: 20 pipes and 2 cubes in a double line on the High West Street side of the bridge across from the public lavatories at the White Hart Inn and the Noah's Ark Inn.

30. Weymouth Avenue: 13 pipes and 14 cubes in a double line at the old entrance to the Southern Railway.

Whilst recording these sites in a letter dated 14 November 1940 from the Borough Surveyor, H.D. Strang to the County Surveyor, it was noted that 'the cost of lighting these blocks is approximately 10/- (ten shillings) per week'.

This completed Phase I of the construction of dragons teeth, but later another 29 sites were chosen and cubes were erected at the following locations:

31. The Grove in West Walks opposite the Castle Inn.
32. Orchard Street at the west end of the road.
33. Grey School Passage at the High West Street end.
34. High East Street by All Saints Church, and by the

Phoenix Inn.

35. London Road by the Labour Hall.

36. St George's Road by Lewis's bakery.

37. Greys Bridge: at both entrances to the bridge. By a Home Defence measure in March 1941 'cratering' was to be charged on 'Action Stations' but it was explained that railway, river and road bridges were only to be blown up as a last resort. I remember watching soldiers of the Royal Engineers boring holes in the haunches of Grey's Bridge in preparation for the placing of charges.

38. London Road by the Exhibition Inn.

39. Prince of Wales Road opposite Aldermans house.

40. Monmouth Road on the corner with Culliford Road railway bridge, by the railway bridge up to 'Chalky Lane'. The bridge also had barbed wire stretched up both sides of the bridge and across the top.

41. Maumbury Road by the entrance to the Great Western Railway goods yard.

42. Weymouth Avenue by the Police Station.

43. South Street: by the Napper's Mite almshouses at the junction with New Street, and by the Westminster Bank in the passageway up to Trinity Street.

44. New Street by Dawes yard.

45. Trinity Street: by what is now Marks and Spencer, by the carrier's yard, in the back of the fire station yard, and by Godwin's china shop.

46. Damers Road by Webbs offices at the approach to Great Western Railway station.

47. Kings Road at Princes Bridge opposite Holloway Road.

48. Maiden Castle Road: on the allotment by the pillbox opposite the gun emplacement situated on the site of the third house in from Florence Road.

49. Southern Railway line from Monmouth Road bridge to Alington Road railway bridge linking with the line of cubes from Monmouth Road railway bridge to the wall by the Dorset War Agriculture Executive Committee building. Another single line of cubes was erected on the actual railway bank from the Monmouth Road railway bridge right through to the Alington Road railway bridge – this would have been just outside the boundary of the allotments, WAEC and Eddisons (by their old fitting shop).

Amazingly 40 of these dragons teeth are still there – from Monmouth Road railway bridge to the boundary of the old intended military hospital – all types – rounded, square and with sloping tops.

50. Alington Road railway bridge. Almost opposite Eddisons old entrance in Alington Road was a track leading up to a building with a tall chimney where the Co-op Dairies kept their lorries. From this path to the railway bridge were a line of dragons teeth. On the actual bridge were a line of holes with concrete plugs to take bent railway line.

51. Southern Railway land near Culliford Road railway bridge. From the Prince of Wales' Road side of Culliford Road railway bridge was a concrete and mesh fence with a gate leading into the SR yard and sidings. Past this gate was a footpath to the SR cottages. Between the footpath and the steep bank of the yard were erected 12 cubes leading down in more or less a straight line, following the bank towards the railway station. They were both of the rounded and square variety and were still there in 1957. There was also a solitary square cube to the north of the 12, by the boundary with Eldridge Pope and Co brewery. Although not now obvious today it was probably placed there to block an open space that existed at the time.

52. Southern Railway sidings. Between the dragons teeth in the previous entry and the station itself, was another single line of 16 square cubes. They were positioned alongside one of the sidings from a point at the end of the last of the cottage gardens/allotments to just short of the old disused cattle pens.

53. Southern Railway. Almost forming a continuous line with those mentioned was a further single line of cubes on a raised piece of ground, just inside the boundary with Eldridge Pope & Co, past the railway engine sheds towards the station.

ROAD BLOCKS

There does not appear to be many records of this type of defence in Dorchester but an official letter dated September 1941 noted that the lighting of the road block at Monmouth Road and London Road (the White Hart) were to be dispensed with. In June 1942 Lt Col C.D. Drew, CO 2nd (Dorchester) Bn Home Guard wrote to the Dorset County Council on behalf of the HQ 114 Infantry Brigade to enquire whether the concrete caps of the sockets for the bent rails of road block were standing up to the weight of traffic. A report by the Town Clerk headed 'Anti tank road block' of November 1942 noted that Mr R.P. Lee of 50 Louise Road was cycling in Damers Road, near the railway bridge, when he was injured by part of the road block, causing £2 worth of damage to his bike: one of the concrete blocks which sealed up the end of the pipe had been displaced. Obviously,

although these defences never caused problems to the Germans they certainly did to the residents of Dorchester!

PILLBOXES

I have been unable to find any official references to Dorchester's pillboxes and all my information has come from people who were resident in the town during the war.

The locations were as follows:

1. Maen, Culliford Road. This was built just inside the stone boundary wall of Maen in Prince of Wales' Road just beyond the junction with Culliford Road railway bridge. Able to fire at the bridge and help protect the dragons teeth along the Southern Railway sidings. Constructed of brick and concrete and protected by earth, it is still there today.

2. Corner of Culliford Road and Prince of Wales' Road. Similar in construction to the one in Maen, this pillbox was built partly underground and also provided fire to the railway bridge and protection to the dragons teeth at the entrance to the Southern Railway yard. The top part has been demolished but the rest remains, albeit covered by soil.

3. Kings Road. Opposite the entrance to Alfred

The remains of the pillbox behind the boundary wall of Maen, at the junction of Prince of Wales Road and Culliford Road North. Together with a second pillbox on the opposite corner, it was intended to stem an advance over Culliford Road Bridge.

Place, No 11 Kings Road juts out into the road, and this formed part of the pillbox built there. The top was covered with barbed wire. Covering fire could be provided up Kings Road toward Prince of Wales' Road, the junction with Icen Way and in the other direction to the area at the bottom of High Street Fordington.

4, 5. By Alington Road Railway Bridge almost opposite Eddisons' entrance in Alington Road was a track leading up to the Co-op building and between the track and the railway line was a strip of land used as allotments. (The entrance gate is still there.) On this, I have been told, were 2 pillboxes, one next to the Alington Road railway bridge known locally as Wareham Bridge and the other near the next bridge on the up-line from Weymouth to Waterloo. (leading down to St George's Road). The pillbox next to the Alington Road railway bridge had a wide field of fire. However, one person who, as a child lived and played near there and another who worked at Eddisons are adamant that neither pillbox was ever there.

6. Maumbury Road. This pillbox was situated between Grasby's old premises and a row of garages before the terrace of houses. Ideally situated to protect both the Maumbury Road and Weymouth Avenue railway bridges.

7. Weymouth Avenue located at the tip of the triangle of land formed by Weymouth Avenue, Maumbury road and the entrance to Little Fairfield, well situated to defend the Weymouth Avenue railway bridge and Maumbury Road.

8. Maiden Castle Road. Opposite the third house in from Florence Road was a pill box by the allotments. This protected the gun that was opposite and provided a wide view over Maiden Castle.

9. Bridport Road. On the top of the railway bank running from Bridport Road railway bridge towards the Great Western Railway station, on the Bridport Villas side. The pillbox is still there, but covered over by brambles and not visible from the bridge or road because of the dense trees. During the war there were no trees and there would have been a clear field of fire, not only towards the railway station but also to cover the bridge and dragons teeth situated there.

10. Bridport Road. On the opposite side of the road to the pillbox listed under number 9, was a similar one, positioned in the corner of the Depot Barracks parade ground bordering Bridport Road and the railway embankment. Dug well in, only the top was visible above ground, giving good fire towards the pillbox opposite, both up and down Bridport Road and across open fields where the hospital now stands. The actual railway bridge was prepared for demolition and there were the usual holes on the bridge itself into which bent railway lines would have been inserted.

11. Poundbury Road. At the opposite end of the Depot Barracks parade ground in the extreme corner bordering Poundbury Road and the railway embankment. This gave covering fire towards the pillbox at the Bridport Road end (see under No 10), as well as giving a good field of fire up and down Poundbury Road and across to Poundbury Camp. The pillbox was not the usual shape, but round.

12. The Grove (I). Where Colliton Walks begins to bend round into Northernhay there are steps leading down to The Grove. Just past these and on the actual bend about three-quarters of the way up from the road was situated a concrete pillbox. Ideally sited to provide a wide field of fire over both bridges over the River Frome, the roads to Yeovil, Sherborne and across the water meadows to Hangmans Cottage.

13. The Grove (II). Just opposite the pillbox described under No 12 was a public house known as The Compasses (now a garage). The cellar was converted into a pillbox with the firing slits about a foot above ground level. Apart from not being able to fire up The Grove, it had the same wide range of fire as the pillbox opposite.

14. Damers Road/Bridport Road. At the apex of the triangle formed by the junction of Damers and Bridport roads was, in 1939, a large house and at the farthest end of their garden a pillbox provided a field of fire up the Bridport road towards the wireless station, as well as covering both sides of both Damers and Bridport roads which, in those days, were open fields. The house was later demolished to make room for flats but some of the concrete and brickwork still remain after the pillbox was broken up.

15. Damers Road. Between Marie Road and Alice Road, in Damers Road where the present school is situated a pillbox gave a field of fire both up and down Damers Road, covering the junction of both Alice and Marie roads and also across open ground to the Bridport road.

16. London Road. Opposite the Exhibition Hotel in London Road, on allotments right next to the path by the River Frome leading to Hangmans Cottage, was a pillbox giving a good range of fire along London Road towards Greys Bridge, up High East Street, the junction with Fordington Hill and across the watermeadows towards Blue Bridge.

17. Greys Bridge. Greys Bridge itself was prepared for blowing up and on the actual bridge were the usual holes, filled with concrete plugs into which bent railway lines could be inserted. These obstructions were provided with covering fire from a pillbox built in the field, just over the bridge by the river bank of the River Frome, on the right hand side towards Kingston Maurward. There was also good all round fire power over the adjacent fields.

18. Blue Bridge. From Hangmans Cottage there is a path which leads to Blue Bridge and once over the bridge there are fields both sides. In the middle of the field on the right hand side towards Frome Whitchurch a pillbox was in a superb position to give an all round range of fire.

19, 20. Wareham Road. On the Wareham Road, past Max Gate, the road used to split, the left fork along Long Lane towards West Stafford and the right fork towards Wareham. On all sides were open fields and on the high bank as the road entered Long Lane was one pillbox whilst on the lower corner opposite was another, both giving good all round cover. The road in between the two pillboxes was prepared for the insertion of bent railway lines.

21. Holloway Road. Just past the entrance to Pound Lane, on the opposite side of the road just before the cottages is a slope leading down to Mill Street. On this slope was a pillbox, half covered with sand bags. Locals firmly believed it was haunted!

22. Colliton Walks. From Top O'Town before the steps leading down to The Grove, as mentioned under number 12, commanding a good field of fire across the roads to Yeovil and Sherborne. Access was from a vertical shaft reminiscent of those used in mine shafts.

Some of the above pillboxes were manned by Regular soldiers whilst others were manned by the local Dorchester Home Guard. It is known that for a time those pillboxes listed under numbers 9-13 inclusive were manned by soldiers from the Dorsetshire Regiment stationed in their depot at The Keep.

All the main roads into Dorchester had obstacles of various kinds, usually of wood and barbed wire construction manned by the Home Guard. All were prepared for cratering, soldiers from the Royal Engineers placing mined charges and borehole charges on their surfaces.

Writing about these pillboxes reminds me of an amusing incident. Early in 1940 I was woken early by the sound of tracked vehicles outside our house in Monmouth Road, directly opposite the 2 pillboxes in Prince of Wales' Road. They were Bren gun carriers, manned by soldiers from the Northumberland Fusiliers, stationed at Blandford Camp. On this particular occasion they were representing 'the enemy' in an anti-invasion exercise, and all their vehicles and helmets bore a white cross. I remember wondering why, if 'the enemy' was Germany, their painted signs were not swastikas and was told that the authorities thought that this might mislead Dorchester folk into thinking the real invasion had started!

For the purposes of the exercise, Dorchester was being defended by soldiers from 'The Dorsets', who were manning the 2 pillboxes. Before the attack started, my mother opened a bedroom window and dropped a bag of flour right into the centre of the Bren gun carrier outside our house. Flour went everywhere and the sergeant in charge – covered in flour – enquired in words peppered with expletives – what she thought she was doing. My mother replied that it represented a home-made Molotov cocktail. Unfortunately for the crew, an umpire complete with white arm band had witnessed the incident and without hesitation marked the vehicle as 'destroyed' and sent it back to Blandford Camp! One nil to the Dorsets!

ANTI AIRCRAFT GUN AND SEARCHLIGHT SITES

The two main guns used by British AA batteries during the war were the 3.7" and the 40mm Bofors and both were used in and around Dorchester. The heavier 3.7", although mobile, was usually dug into a gun emplacement 'gun port' whereas the much lighter Bofors were provided with simple fieldwork dugouts making use of concrete blocks or similar material.

During the early days, the guns came under the control of the 8 AA Division and many will recall that under their red and navy Royal Artillery shoulder title they wore their own individual formation sign – a black German bomber nose – diving earthwards with an 8 pointed red star, representing a shell burst, superimposed on the fuselage, all on a light blue background. Several Heavy Anti Aircraft (HAA) regiments helped man their defences, including the 6th, 92nd and 104th.

The only Light Anti Aircraft (LAA) regiment I have been able to locate is the 14th (West Lothian, Royal Scots) LAA Regiment, RA (TA) who were formed in Scotland in 1938. They were stationed with their Bofors guns on the outskirts of Dorchester near the Broadmayne Road primarily to defend RAF Station Warmwell. They remained there from 1940 until they went to North Africa in 1941.

Searchlight sites were manned by soldiers from the 2nd Searchlight Regiment, 64th AA Brigade Royal Artillery with their HQ at Boveridge House, Cranborne. Their formation sign was a red segment representing a searchlight beam on a dark blue circle.

Later in the war when Dorchester became a base for US troops, their Bofors guns were manned by soldiers from the 204 AAA Battalion, 118 AAA Group and also from the 486th AAA Battalion.

The following sites have been located:

1. Cokers Frome Farm. Past Greys Bridge on the road out of Dorchester is a left turn onto the B3143 towards Piddlehinton. In the field on the left, before Lovers Lane, was a 3.7" AA gun dug into a gun emplacement. There is now no trace of the emplacement but the present farmer, John Mayo, tells me that there was a high mound of gravel in front of the dug out and when the field is ploughed gravel still comes to the surface, thus exactly marking the siting.

2. Exhibition Field. Further up the B3143 (Slyers Lane) just past the turning to Lovers Lane, the field on the right hand side also, for a short time only, had a 3.7 AA gun manned by British troops. Later it was replaced with a searchlight battery and even later by a Bofors gun manned by US troops.

Further along from the guns/searchlight but still in Exhibition Field were army tents to accommodate the crews.

3. Between Dorchester Grammar School and Wareham Road. From the Dorchester Grammar School, there was a narrow path leading past the old cricket pavilion, past the trees and railing that marked the playing field boundary and into open fields and thence to the Wareham Road. On the left hand side was a long stone wall, behind which were farm buildings and opposite the wall, almost at the Wareham Road, was an AA gun site. The first troops to man it were British and the AA weapon was a Bofors gun. Several people remember how unfriendly they were and you were certainly not encouraged to go anywhere near the site. The crew were accommodated in army tents and got their food supplies from the nearby farm. Later the site was taken over by US soldiers from the 204th AAA Battalion also using a Bofors gun. They were much more friendly and supplied the local children with candy and gum.

4. Eddisons Yard. For a while there was a Bofors gun, manned by British troops positioned in the steamrolling yard. Several people can remember it being fired at enemy aircraft.

5. Manor Road/Herringston Road. During the war period, the houses in Manor Road ended about half way down the present road, from South Court Avenue and the road then went into a dirt track, lined by trees on both sides and open fields beyond. Towards the Herringston Road end was, on the left hand side, a path leading to a searchlight site, manned by British troops, partly on the allotments in Herringston Road. It was still there at the end of the war and many local residents joined the crew in a VE day celebration party.

6. Poundbury. Both the British and US troops (204 AAA Battalion from April 1944) manned Bofors guns positioned on top of the Great Western Railway tunnel at Poundbury. The US also had a Bofors gun only a few yards from the Royal Observer Corps post. There were also searchlight sites from time to time.

7. The Modern School. Positioned on the far end of the playing field at the old Modern School was a Bofors gun manned by US troops. Pupils would sing the US national anthem each morning whilst the gun was there.

As well as the 3.7" and 40mm guns there were also much heavier guns positioned in Dorchester.

8. Maiden Castle Road. On the site of the present third house in from Florence Road, in Maiden Castle Road was a large 9.2" howitzer. It had a concrete base with timber cladding and a timber roof to give the appearance, from the air, of an ordinary private house. It had the range to fire over Maiden Castle and into the Channel and was manned by British troops billeted in the Cornwall Hotel. Police would advise local householders when the gun was to be fired in practice so that they could open their windows. The gun was eventually moved, the structure demolished and the land returned to private housing.

9. 'Stinky' Bridge, Weymouth Avenue. Situated in the saw mills, near 'Stinky Bridge' was another 9.2" howitzer, also with the range to reach the English Channel. Again police would advise local householders when it was to be fired in practice. The soldiers manning the gun were housed in Nissen huts in the old football ground. Other Nissen huts alongside were used to house their stores and equipment. There were other Nissen huts on the 'Rec' but whether they were used by the army is not known. Some were there until quite recently and I remember the groundsman, Jack Wilding, keeping his grass cutters in one. They were down at the 'Stinky Bridge' end of the Rec whilst along the Weymouth Avenue side were a row of creosoted wooden huts used by the police during their annual sports days. Again whether these were used by the Army is not known.

10. Maiden Castle Farm. A 9.2" gun was located on the farm property.

11. Maiden Castle Road. For a short time only, a 6' naval gun was located in quite a few different places in the fields along Maiden Castle Road. It had large iron wheels.

12. West Walks. Between the steps leading down to the Grove and Hangmans Cottage dug into the steep

banks of the Walks at Northernhay, was a gun site, capable of firing across to Poundbury and the River Frome.

13. West Walks. At the top of the Grove, in the actual West Walks itself, just before the Thomas Hardy monument and roughly where the present entrance to the library is, was a Hotchkiss gun on wheels.

In addition to the above permanent sites there were, of course, many mobile guns (usually the 40mm Bofors) stationed all around the town for short periods when various troop units were stationed in Dorchester, or merely passing through. This was certainly so in the weeks prior to D-Day. I remember Bofors guns on Maumbury Rings and just off Queen's Avenue. All roads were packed with military vehicles and most had heavy machine guns mounted on them.

Just before D-Day, the air raid siren sounded and every gun opened fire. The sight was amazing, with tracer bullets criss-crossing and Dorchester resembling a gigantic firework display. This together with shell bursts and searchlights filling the sky created an unforgettable spectacle. Unfortunately the Americans enthusiasm was not matched by their discipline: they just opened fire without being told and the result was they shot down two aeroplanes, tragically both Allied aircraft.

14. Little Fairfield. Certainly there was an AA gun in the little triangle of land formed from the junction of Weymouth Avenue, Maumbury Road and the entrance road to Little Fairfield, and described to me as 'the bit of land where 'Dicky' Burden kept his goats' ! A former resident in Maumbury Road described it as a 'heavy gun' and on the few times it was fired, ornaments fell off the sideboard. The fact that it was not 'dug in' , and only protected by sand bags and manned by American troops, suggests it was a heavy but mobile US AA gun.

Apart from lighting up enemy aircraft, the searchlights also had another purpose. On more than one occasion Dorchester saw them being used at night to guide our own damaged or lost aircraft back to the safety of Warmwell aerodrome.

After the war, statistics revealed just how few enemy aircraft were brought down by AA gun fire but from a morale point of view it was very reassuring to hear the guns and see the shells bursting in the sky.

ANTI-GLIDER DEFENCES

In early 1940, the Borough of Dorchester issued an order headed 'Enemy Aeroplane Troops' which included the erection of 8ft wooden poles, 40 yards apart in fields around the town. In a few cases, wire was erected between the poles. These were to impede the landing of German gliders and their airborne troops.

Some specific sites were given – 40 acres Slyers Lane, fields where Melstock Avenue now stands, Maiden Castle Farm, Dirdingle fields, Maiden Castle and Poundbury Farm.

BARRAGE BALLOONS

Although there were no barrage balloons in Dorchester itself, they could be seen, from the Damers Road area, protecting the Royal Naval Air Station at Yeovilton and the Westland Aeroplane works in Yeovil. They were often seen passing through Dorchester, on low loaders – no one was supposed to see them but they were very difficult to camouflage!

OBSERVER CORPS

By the summer of 1940, Britain was covered with observation posts manned by part-time civilians who charted the height and course of enemy aeroplanes, telephoning their sightings to RAF fighter stations. One such post was established on the embankment of the hillfort at Poundbury, made of old railway sleepers and sandbags (part still remains today). The post was machine-gunned by a German aircraft on the 13th of January 1941 without causing injury. Their control centre was at Yeovil (Number 9 Group) and their RAF fighter station was at RAF Warmwell, just outside Dorchester. Mr John Norman was Chief Observer and I recall another member was Mr Joe Wynn from Lloyds Bank. Their rest hut was in the Butts at Poundbury. They wore a distinctive beret with badge and were issued with a rifle and ammunition. In the event of an invasion, the post was to be withdrawn within the protected area of Dorchester and re-positioned on the top of The Keep in Bridport Road.

Early in 1944, three members of the Corps (it

A series of four photographs of the Observer Corps post on the embankment at Poundbury. The post was manned by local men, and their principal task was to identify all planes and pass on the relevant information to their Control Centre in Yeovil. The post was machine-gunned by a German fighter in January 1941, but there were no casualties.

Above A member of the Corps having a fry up.
Above right A general view of the post.
Right Practising aircraft recognition.
Below The post in winter.

became 'Royal' on the 11th April 1941), Alfie Houghton, 'Sailor' Rogers and V. Smith went 'seaborne' with defence ships of the invasion fleet to help identify friendly from enemy aircraft.

STATIC WATER TANKS

Obviously if bombs, especially incendiary bombs, were dropped on Dorchester, a plentiful supply of water would be required to put out the resulting fires. Where main supplies were not considered sufficient to meet these requirements, supplementary water supplies were to be provided by the Home Office. These were black steel dams built to hold a minimum of 5000 gallons of water.

I have been unable to find any official location maps for these tanks but below are listed the ones that can be remembered:

1. The Borough Gardens. Probably the best-remembered water tank was a black rectangular shaped one situated where the later children's paddling pool was located. During the many 'war collection weeks', a rubber dinghy would be floated in the tank, with an effigy of Adolf Hitler at which onlookers were encouraged to throw coins.

2. Maud Road. A round water tank was situated where the old Maud Road School was sited, on the corner of Maud Road and Edward Road.

3. Palace Cinema. This round static water tank was at the side of the cinema next to the iron fire escape steps that went up the side to a door on the top. Children used to climb the steps and throw various objects into the tank much to the annoyance of both the cinema staff and the firemen who had to clear them out.

In Icen Way on the corner with High East Street – opposite where Goulds used to have their shop – there was, until quite recently, a sign in the shape of an arm on the wall indicating where the Palace Cinema water tank was. It said 'NFS' and underneath 'WATER' and underneath again '10,000 GALLS, 486 FEET'.

4. Southern Railway Station Yard. The water tank, built on stilts was situated in the yard, quite near the old Weymouth Avenue entrance where coal merchant G. Bryer-Ash kept his coal stocks.

5. Strouds Gardens. The largest water tank in Dorchester, built in the garden of Strouds South Street shop, between Greyhound Passage and yard and Charles Street (now occupied by Waitrose).

6. Chalky Lane. A large square water tank was built at the Culliford Road end of Chalky Lane on a grass triangle where the lane divided into two paths, one to Culliford Road and the other to the Grammar School. The third side was a plantation of trees.

7. Alexandra Terrace. From Trinity Street a path leads up to Alexandra Terrace and at the top as it rounds the corner outside the boundary wall of the old Somerleigh Court was sited a black water tank.

8. Poundbury. Just before the railway bridge in Poundbury Road, on the right hand side was a small triangle of grass with a path alongside leading to an iron gate giving entrance to Poundbury. A static water tank was built on this triangle of grass.

9. Trinity Street. In the old carriers yard next to the fire station, at the far end from Trinity Street were 2 large static water tanks.

10. The Market. Another of the static water tanks built on stilts, situated by the entrance to Maumbury Road, upon which the present café stands.

11. Holy Trinity Church Grounds. In the passage from High West Street to Colliton Street, Grey School Passage, on the right hand side, in the grounds of Holy Trinity Church (roughly at the back of Thurmans) was a round static water tank.

12. All Saints Church. In the churchyard behind the church in High East Street.

13. Dorchester Recreation Ground, Weymouth Avenue, in the far corner near 'Stinky Bridge'.

14. South Walks. At the South Street end, almost opposite the windows of James Foot Ltd that was actually in South Walks, just past the Cenotaph and before the Air Raid Shelter on the opposite side.

Before the war there were underground water reserves, usually in brick/cement storage tanks with visible covers and connected to the mains supply. They remained empty until required, when the fire brigade would knock out the 'bung' and the tank would fill and provide water for the fire hoses. The only one I have located was opposite the Sydney Arms in Bridport Road and was used during the war in the same way as the above ground static water tank.

At the beginning of the war apprentices from Lott and Walne refurbished and repaired the water well under the Town Pump. This was then used as an emergency water supply to be used if enemy bombs dropped near the centre of the town.

As well as these static water tanks, pipes were laid along the gutters of the main streets of Dorchester. Coming from the river by the White

Hart Hotel, they came up High East Street and thence into High West Street whilst others went underground at the road junction with South Street and Trinity Street. At intervals there were surface water hydrants to which fire pumps could be linked. Not only the main streets were given these pipes; certainly the Cambridge Road area also had them, possibly to make up for the lack of static water tanks in the Park area.

The Dorchester Fire Brigade came under the Borough of Dorchester with headquarters in Princes Street. It became part of the Auxiliary Fire Service (AFS) in 1941 and then the National Fire Service (NFS). They erected signs to help direct fire crews from other local stations – EWS (Emergency Water Supply) and SWS (Station Water Supply).

FURTHER PREPARATIONS

In most southern towns where the German invasion was expected a direct telephone line was installed from a secret location to Whitehall. Its purpose was to pass on information, especially after the Germans had occupied Dorchester, detailing the units involved and their strengths. In Dorchester the location was the conservatory of the premises occupied by Percy Crabb (of motor dealers, Crabb & Co) in Trinity Street (long since demolished).

Two members of the Observer Corps at their post on Poundbury, probably photographed following the issue of rifles.

Preparation against the expected German aerial attacks continued and a repair depot was established at the County Store, King's Road, for repairing gas masks, the clothing of the ARP Service and the equipment of the various fire brigades in the county. Mr W.H. Letheren, Staff Officer for the Rescue and Decontamination Service was placed in charge.

Recruitment for ARP service continued and those that were not old enough to qualify became Air Raid Messengers. Three, amongst the many, were Kathleen Bascombe, Eileen Voss and Marion Dunford – they wore ARP wardens uniforms complete with tin hats and reported twice a week to Tilleys in Trinity Street which was their HQ – Mr Percy Thomas who worked for Tillleys, was in charge. They took food with them – provided they had enough coupons! – slept there and received 2/6 a night. Some manned the telephone exchange whilst others were provided with bicycles.

For the actual ARP personnel it was decided to introduce a warning system. A yellow message (ceased 28 October 1940) called for personnel to be prepared for a possible raid, purple meant 'stand by' and red meant 'imminent attack – sirens to be sounded'. After a raid, a green message was sent (ceased 10 July 1940) which meant 'Raid over but still stand by' and a white message meant 'Stand Down'. I remember seeing an ARP notice at their HQ, 'Aircraft passing overhead this afternoon – don't be alarmed – they are British'. Many training exercises were carried out during this 'phoney war' period. General training was carried out at Louds Mill, by the sewerage works and on Sunday morning, personnel would don protective clothing and climb up and down Maiden Castle – with their gas masks on – as training against a gas attack. Then the journey back to Dorchester for decontamination.

One edition of the *Dorset County Chronicle* carried the headlines 'Dorchester had an air raid last Monday', which was misleading as it referred to a rehearsal only! The 'raid' was preceded by a warning received in the ARP HQ in North Square and the 'attack' included the destruction of Damers Road railway bridge, damage to the bridge area and houses in Maumbury Road and Weymouth Avenue – all with plenty of 'casualties'.

I remember another mock attack when planes from nearby Warmwell bombed the Southern Railway station, using 'bombs' containing flour. The exercise was called 'Lion Door' and I remember it took place on a Sunday morning. It may have been a mock attack, but it seemed realistic, with actual aeroplanes, 'bombs' and 'casualties' complete with red ink bandages. The planes certainly came in very low and one Spitfire caused minor damage to St Mary's church.

Another mock attack, which certainly will be remembered by the then staff of Marks and Spencer, took place – absolutely unannounced and without any warning whatsoever – one Saturday afternoon. Tear gas grenades were tossed into South Street shops. The Marks and Spencer manageress recalls staff and shoppers, with tears streaming down their faces, being ushered onto the store roof and into fresh air. Many shoppers were unable to speak for some considerable time. The store was closed for 3 days and even then there were traces of the gas. The staff had taken their gas masks to the store but left them in the staff room. When questioned, the authorities replied that if they had had their gas masks with them – as required by law – no harm

would have been done. A hard lesson to learn!

In order not to help the enemy in any way once they had landed, maps were cut out of directories in public telephone boxes and all road signs including signposts and milestones were removed. Two areas proved difficult to overcome, local names on drain covers and information on the War Memorial. With the exception of the blackout the removal of these signs probably caused more annoyance than any other anti-invasion measure. It was not until May 1943 that they began to be replaced, with all restrictions finally lifted in October 1944.

For those who did have the petrol for their vehicles and got lost in the lanes of nearby villages they were unlikely to receive much help from the local villagers. All strangers were viewed with the utmost suspicion. Dorchester was rife with rumours. One that persisted for a considerable time was that German paratroopers had been dropped in the vicinity dressed as English workmen and some had actually been spotted in Dorchester itself dressed as nuns – our local nuns were fed up by the number of times they were stopped and questioned!

Apart from these rumours there was also a strong feeling – fuelled by government announcements – that the county was filled with fifth columnists. Even those speaking with a pronounced Dorset accent were regarded with suspicion, and many innocent dog walkers were approached by the ever watchful Home Guard.

One report entitled 'Instructions to Roadmen in the event of an attempted Invasion' included the following, 'If orders are given by anyone not known personally, care should be taken to make sure the order is genuine, as it is to be expected that the '5th column' men will be active'. All these rumours were later proved to be just that . . . rumours!

One 'rumour' was denied by a public announcement in the *Echo* of August 1940. This stated that 'Contrary to a report emanating from an outside source giving the impression that we are short of material for the carrying out of air raid repairs, we beg to advise our customers that contradictary to this rumour, we carry large stocks'.

Public land in Dorchester was made available for vegetable growing and allotments. A pre-war hobby became a necessity and every inch was dug and cultivated for vegetables, not only for one's own family but for neighbours and friends who had no garden. Some of the larger houses in town dug up their lawns: one was Winterborne House, where Captain Williams delivered the resulting vegetables to the rear of Marks and Spencer, by pony and trap, often driven by his daughter.

In early 1940 an urgent appeal was made for scrap aluminium for aircraft production, and a committee was set up to organise the collection. The chairman was Miss Chadwick of 22 Queens Avenue and the secretary, Mrs Hallett of 14 St Georges Road. Other members were Mrs K. Abbott, Mrs Bush, Mrs Cornick, Miss Fewitt, Miss Howard, Mrs Hunt, Mrs H. Lock, Mrs Marsden, Mrs Pitfield, Mrs Sheppard, Mrs Tilley and Mrs Voss. Their slogan was 'Send me your pots and pans, send me your aluminium'. Although the Dorchester response was good, this was more of a propaganda exercise than any real attempt to help aircraft production.

At the same time all railings were collected for the war effort by the Borough of Dorchester. In reality, they were never used and simply stored until they were re-erected after the war. Although it was intended to melt them down, little was done and after the war ended, they were found piled high in storage areas. In hindsight this was a wasted effort, but again was more of a propaganda exercise than anything else.

We were all encouraged to send food and clothes parcels to prisoners of war, and women were asked to knit woollen clothes to keep our troops warm: a lasting memory is of how the ladies always appeared to be knitting! Perhaps to get it into a proper perspective, when asked by a war correspondent 'what comforts the troops most missed?' an infantry officer replied, 'the girls we left behind'.

'Make do and mend' became a popular slogan and nothing was ever thrown away. Socks were darned so much that one ended up darning the darns. Pamphlets were published by the Board of Trade containing such helpful items as 'Where's that moth?', 'Unpick and knit again' and 'Decorative patches'. The character used to popularise these pamphlets was Mrs Sew-and-Sew, a thin puppet figure, cotton reel body and clothes peg legs whose particular slogan was 'Mend and made do, to save buying new' and even more hints on 'How to patch elbows or trousers' etc.

IF THE GERMANS HAD LANDED

Although never put to the test, the preparations for the expected invasion were vitally necessary. After the war, captured German documents showed their intended invasion was planned to land between Weymouth and Lyme Regis. Three divisions of Field Marshall Walter Von Reichenau's 6th Army, and part of Field Marshall Fedor Von Brek's Army Group 13 would lead the assault.

After the capture of Weymouth the plan was to thrust northwards and head through Dorchester to the north Dorset downs, consolidate and prepare for an attack on Bristol. In addition, glider-borne troops were to be landed on the outskirts of Dorchester.

SIX

The Battle of Britain
August 8th – October 31st 1940

After Dunkirk, an invasion of this island seemed inevitable. It was obvious to everyone that this would be preceded by the German Luftwaffe attempting to destroy the Royal Air Force. Their attempt and ultimate failure later became known as 'The Battle of Britain'. Officially, this battle lasted from August 8 to the October 31 1940 but, as far as Dorchester was concerned, it ended on October 7 when German bombers attacked the Westland Aircraft Works at nearby Yeovil.

Although this book is, by necessity, confined to Dorchester itself, the nearby aerodrome of Warmwell played such a huge part in the aerial battles over the town during the Battle of Britain that it must be mentioned.

Originally named RAF Woodsford this grass station became RAF Warmwell in July 1938. During the 1939 open Air Day at Warmwell 5 Avro Ansons battled with 3 Hawker Hurricanes before a mock factory was bombed and destroyed. Quite a few of us feared that this might soon become reality. Other aircraft that took part in the display were Hawker Hawks, Fairy Battles, Westland Wallaces, and a Short Singapore flying boat from Calshot. Due to protracted construction works the airfield, intended for forward fighter operations, did not become fully operational until July 1 1940 when it was transferred to Group 10 Fighter Command and manned by Hurricanes of 609 (West Riding) Squadron and Spitfires from 152 (Hyderabad) Squadron. Often joined by Hurricanes from 238 Squadron and Spitfires of 234 (Madras Presidency) Squadron both from RAF Middle Wallop and Hurricanes of 213 Squadron from Exeter, these were the fighter planes that fought the Luftwaffe in the skies over Dorset during that hot summer of 1940.

I was a pupil at Dorchester Grammar School at

A photograph from the Imperial War Museum showing pilots in the crew room at RAF Warmwell. The station played a leading role in the Battle of Britain.

the time, and in a classroom directly facing Warmwell. I could watch the planes taking off, knowing that some 3 minutes later the air raid sirens would sound and we would go to the covered trenches. Next would come the firing of shells from the local anti-aircraft batteries and the quite distinct drone of the German aircraft. Cotton wool-like puffs of smoke would appear where the shells burst. Often accompanied by German fighter aircraft they would be seen high in the sky as small silver specks, easily identified by the long white vapour trails that billowed out behind them.

The anti-aircraft guns would cease firing and the defending Spitfires and Hurricanes would attack. Suddenly the orderly vapour trails became much less orderly as the bombers took evasive action and the sky was filled with machine-gun fire from both the attackers and the defenders. The whole sky filled with criss-cross vapour trails

and the distant sounds of battle.

Planes would fall out of the sky, trailing black smoke, and you would pray that they were Germans and not British. One watched to see if any parachutes would suddenly open up. Single ones meant a fighter pilot, several meant a bomber and that had to be German.

There were occasions when one froze in horror as a British pilot drifting down to the ground beneath his parachute canopy would be machine gunned by a German fighter – this was total war! After one such incident when a Messerschmitt 109 machine gunned and killed a British pilot who had bailed out another Messerschmitt 109 was shot down. Although its pilot got out of the cockpit, his parachute failed to open and people cheered as he plunged to earth: some even went to look at the depression in the ground where he had fallen on the Wareham Road. One really had to have lived through the war to appreciate and understand the intense feelings of hate towards Hitler and his Nazis.

Having counted the aircraft taking off from Warmwell, we counted them back, hoping against hope that the two counts would tally. After the attack was over and the 'all clear' had sounded, we searched for spent machine gun bullets, shrapnel and pieces of aircraft. I still have some 'souvenirs'.

Dogfights over Dorchester became a daily occurance and one I remember took place on July 4th 1940 when 90 Junker JU 87s flew fairly low

Its quality may be poor, but this rare and dramatic photograph shows a German Messerschmitt ME 109 passing to the right of the Barracks entrance (now the Military Museum) in 1940. The plane to the left was a Hurricane. The photograph was taken from the Observer Corps post at Poundbury and was given to Dorset County Museum by Jim Foot.

over the town to attack a convoy of ships off Portland, later attacking the harbour and sinking an AA ship, HMS *Foylebank*. One could clearly see from Dorchester the clouds of dense black smoke rising from naval fuel tanks that had been hit and set on fire.

Two particular incidents are etched forever in my memory, both in 1940, at the height of the Battle of Britain. The first took place on August 13, 'Eagle Day' or 'Adlertag', when the Luftwaffe atttacked military targets in southern England with almost 300 aircraft.

I remember seeing Warmwell's Spitfires take off, followed soon afterwards by the inevitable air raid warning sirens. They were joined by Hurricanes of 238 Squadron from Middle Wallop. Some time elapsed before I saw the German planes over Dorchester – they were Junkers JU87 dive bombers. All dive-bombers made a screech as they dive bombed, but the Junkers JU87, known as the 'Stuka', was fitted with sirens and the noise when they dived was quite terrifying: I had often heard them when they had attacked ships in Portland Harbour.

A Spitfire on the ground at RAF Warmwell. This is thought to be the Spitfire that made a forced landing near Maiden Castle Farm in August 1940.

Records show that there were 27 Stukas in this particular raid and they were on the way to their target, RAF Middle Wallop north of Salisbury. The German aircraft were flying much lower than usual and were easily recognisable by the markings on the fuselage, wings and tail. The battle raged over Dorchester. At four o'clock in the afternoon I saw a Stuka shot down by a Spitfire. A friend and I quickly got out our bicycles and pedalled off in the direction of the crashed plane, which had dense black smoke coming from it. We found it at Grimstone near the viaduct, some 200 yards from the railway station. Although the official report said it was totally wrecked, I disagree. Certainly the nose of the plane was embedded in the soil but the rest was intact. Both airmen were quite visible, both dead. A 600lb unexploded bomb lay on the ground beside the plane. We were the first two people to find it and we were able to obtain a piece of the plastic cockpit before the Army and RAF personnel arrived to prevent people doing just that (and yes, I still have the piece of cockpit!).

The two crew were later identified as Feldwebel Erich Haach from Krassen and Gefreiter Heinrich Myer from Oberhausen and they were buried in graves with wooden crosses at the side of the road bordering the field in which they crashed. In the late 1960s their bodies were removed and reburied in a military cemetery.

The second memory, also in the skies above Dorchester, took place the following month on Sunday September 15. The Spitfires of 152 (Hyderabad) Squadron had been 'scrambled' from Warmwell, and as usual, whilst my father took shelter indoors, my mother and I rushed out into the garden to see what was happening. The roar from the engines of the German bombers, which was distinctive and quite different from English aircraft engines, became louder and louder – far louder than we had ever heard before, but we were unable to spot them. This was because they had crossed low over the coast to get under the radar warning system. The noise of their engines became deafening. Suddenly they appeared over the rooftops of Monmouth Road. They were so low I really thought they would hit the chimney pots: I have never seen aeroplanes that low, before or since. Every detail could be seen, not only the planes' markings and numbers but the expressions on the crews' faces. Despite the shock my mother and I were still able to give them the famous Churchill V for Victory sign with our fingers . . . their expressions did not change at all!

The German aircraft were 30 Heinkel HE 111 bombers of Kampfgruppe SS from Chartres. As they flew off toward Portland one solitary Spitfire attacked from behind and there were several bursts of machine gun fire. Later official reports confirm that at least one Heinkel was shot down,

but at the time all we had to go on was the 'Victory Roll' carried out by one of the returning Spitfires. These 'Victory Rolls' were frowned on as they endangered both the pilot and the plane, but the pilots did them anyway!

I remember two of our Spitfires crashing, one after being shot down over Dorchester by a German ME 109 (records show this was from 602 squadron on August 25 1940) and the other from 152 squadron based at RAF Warmwell, when the pilot lost control.

The heroes of that summer, the pilots and aircrews of Fighter Command, were a familiar and popular sight. They drove round Dorchester in battered sports cars (they always had enough petrol!), with scarves tucked into their flying jackets – full of life and fun with their 'live for today' attitude. And how young they were.

Although their unofficial 'drinking-hole' was the Frampton Arms at Moreton, their favourite pub near Dorchester was the Sun at Charminster. I wonder if the fact that this was also popular with the Womens Land Army girls had anything to do with it?

The residents of Dorchester soon got used to RAF slang. Their aeroplanes were 'kites' , their hangers 'sheds', and the Nissen huts in which they lived, 'iron lungs'. A flight across the Channel was 'over the ditch' and dropping bombs were 'laying eggs'. A crash was 'a prang' and they used phrases such as 'jolly good show, chaps'. But they paid a high price for their courage and bravado,

This photograph of a training exercise known as 'Queen 2' shows two Blenheim bombers flying low over the town in 1940.

immortalised in Prime Minister Winston Churchill's words: 'Never in the field of human conflict was so much, owed by so many, to so few.'

On September 26 1943 there was a parade in Dorchester to commemorate 'The Few'. A regimental band led the parade that included the RAF, WAAF, ATC and soldiers from local A-A batteries and the ROC. The salute was taken by a Battle of Britain pilot, Wing Commander A.G. Douglas DFC and the parade ended with a service in the Plaza Cinema, conducted by Rev G. Clare-Morrow. The Mayor, Mr K.W. Abbott was in attendance.

AFTER THE BATTLE

After the defensive Battle of Britain phase, which ended in October 1940 when the Luftwaffe switched to bombing cities, Warmwell took over a more offensive role and Dorchester then welcomed the Polish airmen of 302 (Pozanski) Squadron who flew Hawker Hurribombers. Their stay was brief, only 5 weeks, and in November they were replaced by a Canadian Squadron, No 402 (Winnipeg Bear). They also flew Hurribombers. Other Polish airmen flew with various squadrons and I remember in one instance, with their surnames quite unpronouncable, three were known as Zig, Zag and Zog.

In August 1941 a decoy airfield was constructed at Knighton (NGR SY 812 866). Three months later the much loved Westland Lysanders (affectonately nicknamed 'Lizzies') of 276 Squadron were posted to Warmwell, and were soon seen in the skies over Dorchester. We were unaware at the time but one of their tasks was the landing and picking up of Special Operations Executive agents into and from occupied Europe. The squadron also flew Walrus and Anson aircraft. Lysanders often landed and took off at Poundbury – why I do not know – perhaps to liaise with the Observer Corps post there.

Hurribombers returned to Warmwell in March 1942 with 175 Squadron and took part in the ill-fated Dieppe raid. These were followed in 1942 by 263 and 266 (Rhodesia) squadrons with their Westland Whirlwinds and Hawker Typhoons respectively.

In September 1942, Dorchester welcomed Rhodesian airmen, when 266 (Rhodesia) Squadron was based at Warmwell with Hawker Typhoons to counter low level 'tip and run' raids by Fokker Wolf 190s. 1943 saw the arrival of 257 (Burma) Squadron (Typhoons), 263 Squadron (again), 164 (Argentine-British) Squadron (Hurricanes), 263 Squadron (and again) and 257 (Burma) Squadron (Typhoons). Czech, Indian and Canadian airmen amongst others all flew out of Warmwell.

Dorchester was also loosely connected with the famous 'bouncing bombs' during the winter of 1942/3, when prototype bombs were tested at Chesil Beach prior to Guy Gibson's Dambusters Raid, with Warmwell being used as a 'forward base'. The first test took place on December 3 when a Wellington bomber, piloted by Captain Joe' Mutt' Summers dropped a bomb off Chesil Beach. The inventor Barnes Wallis and his team were housed in West Stafford House, West Stafford, from December 1942.

RAF Warmwell was officially handed over to the USAAF in August 1942, but apart from a few occasions for emergency landings it was not until September 1943 that Dorchester saw American planes flying overhead. In March 1944, Warmwell became Station 454 of the USAAF's 9th Air Force

and home to the 474 Fighter Group and the 3 squadrons of Lockheed P38s (Lightnings) based there. Many other American aircraft landed at Warmwell due to lack of fuel or bad weather. They moved to France in August and the airfield was handed back to the RAF, bringing a return of the familiar Spitfires and Typhoons. Spitfires were also used for Air Sea Rescue missions, helped by Walrus aircraft who dropped life rafts.

RAF Warmwell did not escape the attention of the Luftwaffe. The first attack I remember took place on August 25 1940 when, despite intercepted messages announcing an imminent attack being picked up from a German Enigma machine and then decoded at Bletchley Park, the airfield was bombed in the early evening. Aircraft and hangars were damaged, and the sick quarters received a direct hit. The attack lasted some twenty minutes and I remember thinking that this kind of thing should not happen on a Sunday!

Perhaps the worst attack, certainly as far as casualties were concerned, took place on April Fools Day 1941 when, at about 12.30pm, the aerodrome was attacked without warning. 3 Heinkel HE IIIs crossed the coast near Lyme Bay, followed the railway line from Dorchester and dropped some 40 bombs, resulting in 10 RAF and WAAF personnel being killed and many injuried. Aircraft, hangers, offices and workshops were destroyed or damaged. The residents of Dorchester were shocked and saddened by the loss of lives. Many of the dead had been frequent visitors to the town and had forged local friendships.

RAF WARMWELL TODAY.
RAF Warmwell's action days came to an end when in October 1945, it was placed on a 'Care and Maintenance' order. It was officially closed in November. All that now remains of this once proud and vital aerodrome are two former hangers now used for agricultural purposes, part of the control tower now incorporated into a house, and the crumbling remains of a few fighter pens and sundry buildings. Only a visit to the Holy Trinity churchyard and the nearby RAF memorial brings the memories flooding back.

SEVEN

Local Defence Volunteers, Home Guard, Auxiliary Units

After the side-stepping of the Maginot Line by German forces and the retreat of the French, followed by the miraculous evacuation from Dunkirk, France formally surrendered on June 22 1940, leaving Great Britain alone to fight the might of the victorious German army.

Almost a month earlier, the Secretary of State for War, Mr Anthony Eden, broadcast an appeal to the nation, appealing for volunteers to take up arms in defence of their home towns. The following day Dorchester Police Station was jammed by men demanding to join the new force, many of whom had been in the armed forces during the First World War. Some even arrived wearing their medals as evidence of their previous experience.

The new force was to be called the Local Defence Volunteers, or LDV for short, dubbed by the comedian Tommy Trinder as 'Look, Duck and Vanish'! On 31 July 1940 its name was changed to the Home Guard.

In Dorset the organisation and setting up of the LDV was given to Major General Harry Marriott-Smith who reported direct to the War Office. The county was to be covered by 6 battalions. The 2nd Dorset (Dorchester) Battalion was formed in February 1941 under the command of Lieutenant Colonel C.D. Drew DSO, OBE.

Initially, men paraded in their civilian clothes with an armband with the letters LDV. When the name was changed, Home Guard armbands were worn and often these are found with the initial LDV armband beneath the new one.

Gradually, battledress and brown leather gaiters were issued and, as the Dorchester Home Guard were affiliated to the Dorsetshire Regiment, they wore its metal cap badge in their forage caps. Officers wore the same badge but in bronze. On both sleeves of the battledress blouse and the greatcoat they wore the county distinguishing

Colonel C.D. Drew DSO, OBE, commander of the 2nd Dorset (Dorchester) Battalion of the Home Guard, photographed in civilian clothes with a group of American officers outside the Dorset County Museum (of which Colonel Drew was also Curator) in 1944.

letters DOR, with the number 2 below to denote the Dorchester Battalion. Above was worn a Home Guard cloth shoulder title. Unique to the Dorchester Battalion, its members wore a slip-on epaulette between the neck and the shoulder of the battledress blouse, bearing the words HOME GUARD, at the shoulder end. One member tells me that when in 1940 he enlisted and reported to The Keep which was then occupied by the 14th Infantry Training Company, he simply took off his Home Guard insignia and kept the same battledress for the army.

Major Whittaker was the Commanding Officer at the HQ, which was at what was then Mears Store at the junction of Charles Street and South Walks. Parades took place in South Walks with anything that could be used to 'shoulder arms'. There were old muskets, 2.2 rifles, and I even saw broom handles being used for drill at the Grammar School. After the parade units marched

off to their various sentry posts, which included Bincombe Tunnel, the telephone exchange, the railway stations, the water and sewerage works.

In Dorchester, every exit road was manned by the LDV, whose obstacles and barbed wire formed a chicane.

Another unit, commanded by Captain Davis, guarded the post office and the searchlight battery in Herringston Road, where they had to report with bicycles to act as messengers.

The Marconi 'Beam Wireless Station' in Bridport Road, Dochester formed their own Home Guard unit, some 50 strong, the buildings being enveloped in large camouflage nets, brought down one winter night by heavy snow.

NCO's and soldiers of 21 Platoon, 'C' Company, Infantry Training Centre, Poundbury Camp, in 1940.

Local firm, Lott and Walne, also formed their own Home Guard company. When rifles were received in crates from the USA, they found them packed in solid grease, so they were washed and cleaned in an old cattle trough filled with paraffin. Later the assembled rifles were tested at Kingston Maurward before before being issued to other companies.

Mr Brian Toop's father, who worked for the Post Office, was trained to take over the telephone exchange in the event of an invasion, and he was very 'miffed' when the Post Office Home Guard were badged to the Hampshire Regiment and not to the 'Dorsets'. The Post Office had their own Home Guard unit, their C.O. being a Mr Sansom. Sentries were posted at the vehicle entrance to the Post Office in New Street and Mr Toop always wondered why a gap had been left at the top of the

Men working at the Marconi 'Beam Wireless Station' on the Bridport Road. The once familiar masts of the Station were used for transmissions to America, South America, Egypt and the Far East. Despite being singled out by the Germans as a target, the Wireless Station survived unscathed (*see also the aerial photograph on page 68*).

doors as hand grenades could easily have been lobbed over the top. The public side entrance to the Post Office in New Street was closed during the war.

The Eldridge Pope brewery and the Southern Railway also had their own Home Guard, the latter not being formed until later in the war.

Whilst most wartime residents of Dorchester will remember the LDV and Home Guard it will probably come as a surprise that there was also a British Resistance movement in Dorchester.

These were the members of the Dorchester Home Guard who 'volunteered' to join an elite band of civilian soldiers in July 1940. They were picked largely for their intimate knowledge of the area, their ability to get on well with colleagues and for their practical skills. They were trained in the use of explosives, all types of fuses and booby traps. They carried revolvers, tommy-guns and grenades. The Royal Engineers built them 'hides', consisting of underground rooms for the storage

Top-secret auxiliary Resistance units supposed to conceal themselves in underground hides should the Germans invade were stationed throughout Dorset. The hide for the Dorchester unit was in Came Woods, whilst their ammunition and weapons were hidden nearby beneath Culliford Clump, shown on the right.

Men of the Dorchester Home Guard enjoying a drink after training in 1943.

of the explosives and sleeping quarters. The idea was that when the Germans came, they were to 'go to ground' in their concealed shelters, let the enemy pass through and then emerge and do as much damage as they could 'behind the lines'.

There were several such 'hides' in the Dorchester area but the one associated with the town was in Came Woods (grid reference SY 7033 8906), but there are now few traces of the site. About 100 yards in from the central opening along the main road a metal hut was buried 9ft down and covered by foliage and undergrowth. There was a hatch for entering, and enough room to

The 'Stand Down' parade of the 2nd Battalion Dorset (Dorchester) Home Guard in the football field behind the Marabout Barracks, December 1944.

squeeze in nine men: their ammunition and weapons were hidden under Culliford Clump. It was officially described as an 'Auxiliary Unit Operational Base'. Mr 'Bert' Jewell, then working for the Rural District Council, saw the building going on at Culliford Clump and wrote to the MoD asking for rent – but all the MoD were concerned with was how he knew about it!

What was unique about this 'hide' was, unlike most that were constructed by the Royal Engineers, this one was built by soldiers of the Dorsetshire Regiment stationed in the town. Those selected were very secretive about their mission, much to the annoyance of their comrades.

There was another hide at Knowle Hill in the woods near Bradford Peverell.

There was also an 'Auxiliary Unit Special Duties Outstation' under grid reference SY 691 905 and described as 'Somewhere south of the hospital, Dorchester'. From the references this is not the old County Hospital in Prince's Road, but the Isolation Hospital in Herringston Road. Their headquarters was at Duntish Court but they did much of their explosives training at Highworth near Swindon.

Officially known as 'Auxiliary Units, Home Guard', they wore camouflage overalls over their Home Guard uniforms. Perhaps to cause further confusion, they wore the cap badge of the Norfok Regiment. Secrecy was paramount and not even parents, wives or sweethearts know what their loved ones really did. Commanded by a Captain Weaver there is now only one member still alive. Extremely brave men, all of them.

The Home Guard was officially disbanded on 1 November 1944.

EIGHT

Air Raids and Bomb Damage

Although bombs were dropped on Dorchester during the war and there was some machine-gunning there was no planned German raid (confirmed after the war from captured German official records). The bombs that did fall were jettisoned from German aircraft either whilst being attacked on their way to an intended target or on their return, usually when they had been unable to locate their target. Dorchester was on the German flight path to Bristol, Coventry and Exeter. As early as June 1940, residents heard the nightly throb of pulsating Jumo engines from German Heinkels, Junkers and Dorniers, the anti-aircraft fire and the occasional 'whistle and crump' of dropping bombs, and we saw the probing searchlights, coloured tracer bullets and the phospherescence of incendiary bombs.

The local papers rarely mentioned where bombs landed. The reports generally talked about raids in general – whether they were heavy and concentrated or light and widespread. Their headlines would be on the lines of 'Hitlers' raiders attack South Coast Town'. The 'bush telegraph' did work, however, and local bomb locations were usually known to all by the next day.

Bombs dropped on land adjoining Dorchester were officially listed as follows:

12 July 1940. HE at Winterborne Came and Dorchester Weirs, killing a horse.

20 August. 7 HE bombs at Came Down golf links.

3 October. HEs dropped 150yds west of Kellaways Farm, West Stafford. 1 soldier killed and 2 injured.

20 October. HE bomb at Stinsford.

11 November. 2 HE bombs at Winterborne Monkton.

10 January 1941. 500 incendiary bombs at Charminster, probably jettisoned by a German bomber when returning from a raid on Poole.

IN DORCHESTER ITSELF

24 August 1940 (Saturday). At 23.10 2 HE bombs at South Walks Road. These landed in the corner of the field next to South Walks House (now a School). Both exploded, causing some damage to the masonry of the wall bordering the house. No casualties. The story at the time was of a courting couple who were sitting on a bench on the opposite side of the road who disappeared – no one ever found out who they were – perhaps it was an illicit meeting? Houses nearby were evacuated and 2 elderly ladies and their maids were escorted by soldiers to a cellar under one of the banks. Later the same evening all those evacuated were allowed to return to their homes. At 11 o'clock on the next day (Sunday) someone reported the old ladies and maids missing. They were eventually located, none the worse for their ordeal but hungry and thirsty.

25 August 1940 (Sunday). Although decoded signals from a captured Enigma machine warned of an impending attack on RAF Warmwell no evasive action had been planned. Approaching enemy aircraft were spotted at 16.45. 12 Spitfires of 152 Squadron took off half-an-hour later, and at 17.30 the station was attacked by 50 to 70 German bombers. The Spitfires were joined by Hurricanes of 87 Squadron and 213 Squadron from RAF Exeter. Many bombs were dropped on Warmwell and 2 HEs dropped short of the target at Louds Piece, Dorchester, in a field behind Colonel Drew's house. Both had delayed action fuses and one exploded three days later, leaving a crater 40ft in diameter and 25 feet deep. Luckily there were no casualties, although some passing children were covered in chalk and looked like ghosts, and only slight damage to the roof tiles and windows of two nearby houses. The other HE bomb was defused by members of the Royal Engineers' bomb

An aerial photograph taken on the western side of Dorchester by a Luftwaffe Target Reconnaissance aircraft on October 7 1940. The photograph is marked with two targets. In the centre A. GB 4975 is the Wireless Station on the Bridport Road, whilst to the right is Poundbury Camp (B. GB 1461). Neither target was ever bombed.

disposal squad. One local resident remembers a piece of shrapnel embedded itself in one of the kitchen windows in Colonel Drew's house and it was there for years. Colonel Drew was very proud of it and always carefully painted around it! Mr Ernie Coombes was walking with his friend Mr Trevor Brown when the second bomb went off (quite near Colonel Drew's old house – now demolished). Both suffered minor injuries but were part of the casualties statistics! Mary Lock had a pony in a field between Colonel Drew's house and Max Gate and a piece of shrapnel from

the bomb cut the chin of the pony. Although the official records state that two bombs were dropped, local residents saw three and explained the difference by remembering that two bombs dropped at the exact same spot, causing one large crater.

1 October 1940 (Tuesday). 1 HE bomb dropped on an allotment in Dorchester. No other details. No damage or casualties.

12 October 1940 (Saturday), time 21.10. 200 incendiary bombs dropped on open ground and woods between Fordington Farm and Came House causing a number of small fires, quickly brought under control by Dorchester Fire Brigade and the military. There was no serious damage and no casualties. At 21.45 7 HE bombs and 2 oil incendiary bombs were dropped at Winterborne Came near Came House. Again no casualties or damage.

16 October (Wednesday). Cryptanalysts at Bletchley Park, with the aid of the captured Enigma deciphering machine, intercepted a German signal 'Target No 1 for Y'. The code '1' indicated the Armed Fighting Vehicles School at Bovington Camp as the target and the 'Y' indicated that the Germans would be using their Y-beam radar direction signals to enable the bombers to reach their target.

Some bombs dropped short of their target and hit Dorchester at 21.45: 8 HE bombs, 1 oil incendiary bomb and approximately 200 kilo incendiary bombs. All 8 HE bombs failed to explode, not as thought at the time because they were 'duds' but because the Germans had started to use delayed action fuses to cause longer periods of disruption.

They dropped:

In the garden of No 3 Salisbury Villas. The bomb landed in soft ground causing a 12 feet deep hole, leaving no part of the bomb exposed. There were no splinters or windows broken. Nearby houses were evacuated and Salisbury Street closed. When I investigated I found no such place – only numbers 1 and 2. Miss Kathy Bascombe said there never was a number 3. She lived in Salisbury Terrace and remembers the bomb landing in the garden of 3 Salisbury Terrace (occupied and owned by a Mrs Bull). The whole terrace was evacuated and those who could, went to friends or relatives.

12 Harvey Buildings, where the bomb penetrated the roof of a lean-to building and embedded itself in the floor. Nearby houses were evacuated and Fordington High Street and part of Holloway Road were closed. The nearby school was also closed. With the ground being so soft it went deeper and as far as is known it is still somewhere underground – as one 'wag' remarked, 'It's probably slipped down to London Road by now!' Who knows? At the time the house was owned by M.J. Sargeant.

Icen Way, behind Quinton's antique shop, where the bomb embedded itself in the soft earth. Icen Way was closed and adjacent houses evacuated. According to one resident, the actual bomb dropped outside the old Palace Cinema and he and his family were evacuated to the Three Mariners public house in High East Street. There were public air-raid shelters below the pub. One resident was allowed back into the garden of his house to feed the family chickens.

15 Cornwall Road (occupied by Miss Lankshear and E.W. Stirret) in a room at the rear of the house. There was no crater, but houses either side were evacuated whilst Victoria and Cornwall Roads were closed. The site was visited by a bomb disposal squad official and on the 17th the incident was reported cleared and the roads re-opened.

44 London Road, 10 yards south of the A35. Nearby houses were evacuated and the A35 closed from Greys Bridge to the bottom of High East Street. The premises at the time was F. Aldeman's workshops.

Great Western Railway. On the sidings, 100 yards north of the down line signal box causing a hole 2' in diameter and 2' deep embedding itself between 2 sleepers. Rail traffic was stopped between Maiden Newton and Dorchester. By the 17th a bomb disposal squad officer recorded the incident closed.

In *the garden of Holy Trinity rectory*, Princes Street, 50 yards south of the house. Nearby houses in Somerleigh Court were partially evacuated.

Public Assistance Institution, known locally as Damers Road Hospital, or the workhouse, at the rear of the Casual Ward by the chapel. The bomb was fully exposed (approximately 112 lbs) and had struck a stone wall and deflected into the side of the ward. The nearby nurses hostel and wards were evacuated. By the 17th a bomb disposal squad officer had visited the site and declared the incident closed. One resident recalls a postman on his bicycle, near where Gawlers had their premises at the time, on hearing the whine of the falling bomb throwing himself over a front garden wall of one of the nearby houses.

Incendiary bombs also dropped in the area, several in the *Damers Road allotments*, much to the annoyance of one allotment owner who was incensed that he had lost all his onions. One man was actually working on his allotment at the time and several people can remember seeing the bomb drop from the last of the 24 bombers that passed overhead. One householder in Alice Road was seen to place a dustbin lid on an incendiary bomb

Bomb Damage in Dorchester, 1939 – 1945

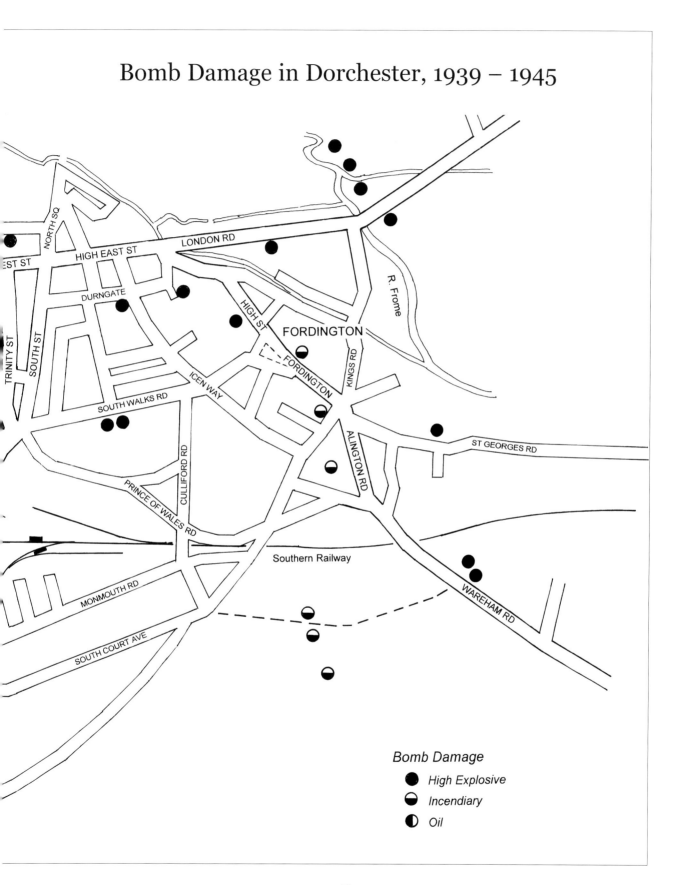

outside his house. When he later went to retrieve it, the bomb suddenly flared up and he fled into the house leaving it to the professionals to extinguish.

An oil incendiary bomb fell in *Trinity Street*, outside the Plaza Cinema. Luckily the bomb did not ignite. If it had exploded it would certainly have taken out the centre of the town. When the bomb disposal squad defused it there was found to be a large quantity of sand in it with a written message 'This is the best we can do for you . . . Czech Resistance'. One wonders where that piece of paper is now? Some damage was caused to nearby shops and windows of houses. Fry's Café opposite the Plaza (wonderful doughnuts) was damaged and for years there was a piece of shrapnel embedded in the 'R' of Fry's. There were no casualties.

At the same time 200 incendiary bombs dropped in the *Victoria Park district*, causing fires in 9 houses. The fires were quickly brought under control by the Dorchester Fire Brigade and members of the AFS. Bombs burning in the fields and roads were quickly extinguished by both police and wardens. Again, no casualties.

18 October 1940 (Friday). An HE bomb dropped at *Greys Bridge*, 200yds from the bridge, 200yds to the east and 50yds south of the A35. There was no crater in the boggy soil, and no casualties.

1 November 1940 (Friday). HEs dropped in the *Victoria Park area* causing craters 4 feet across. 1 bomb fell at the entrance to a house in Treves Road, the other 2 in the same line but in fields. No damage or casualties. Several much smaller bombs also dropped at the same time, landed in the allotments in Damers Road, but did not explode. Whilst these bombs were being dropped, patients in Dorset County Hospital were ordered to get under their beds by the matron!

The sirens sounded on the 15 November 1940 when radar picked up an unidentified aircraft flying in low from the Channel. The plane, a French 2 seater mono plane landed at Hulls Farm, Stinsford, and its pilot and passenger were taken into custody. They later proved to be two Frenchmen who had escaped from occupied France to join General de Gaulle's Free French Forces.

11 December 1940. At 23.55 an enemy plane flying south eastwards over Dorchester machine-gunned the town. Bullets penetrated the roof of a house and others fell on roadways. No casualties.

12 January 1941 (Sunday). Just after midnight an HE bomb exploded in *Poundbury Camp* leaving a crater 12' in diameter and 3' deep. 2 sentries were thrown to the ground from the blast.

Another bomb, which did not explode, was also found in the camp. It was attached to a parachute, which was partly on the Great Western Railway line at Poundbury. On the parachute was stamped 'Littlewood Mail Order Stores Ltd, Parachute Division, 50 Hanover St, Liverpool 1, 8/12/40'. There is no record of the mystery being solved, and it remains as such to this day

13 January 1941. The Observer Corps look out at *Poundbury* was machine-gunned by an enemy plane. No casualties.

12 April 1941 (Saturday). Following an HE and incendiary attack on Upton, to the west of Poole, 2 HE bombs (presumably jettisoned on the return journey to Germany) dropped on open ground at *Maiden Castle*. Both exploded but there was no damage or casualties.

A May 1941 report, relating to Dorset as a whole, stated that air attacks, particularly at night, had been widespread and growing in intensity, with substantial damage and some fatal casualties, especially in the south of the county. Morale of the public remained high and the Civil Defence services had all shown a commendable standard of efficiency.

25 April 1942 (Saturday). 4 HE bombs of 250kg dropped in the *Fordington area*. 3 landed in the water meadows north of the River Frome and exploded, the other landed on the south bank, north of St George's Road. Two houses were rendered uninhabitable and it was thought might have to be demolished. 3 others were uninhabitable but repairable. Superficial damage to 65 other houses. A man and a woman were slightly hurt, but 10 cows and a horse were killed.

Several local residents remember the incident well and recall the bomb in St George's Road falling behind a terrace of houses. An occupant of

As Dorchester increasingly found itself a target, ARP exercises continued. Here a stretcher is being lowered over the river near Grey's Bridge in 1941.

one, a Mr Adams, was in the field behind the houses when the bomb landed. He suffered slight shrapnel wounds to his neck. Another resident remembers a stained glass window on the north side of St George's church being sucked out by the blast.

A report of July 1944 noted two demonstrations of the hazards of butterfly bombs being held at Colliton Park. The first was attended by 250 American officers and men, as well as 50 from the RAF; the second one by 220 Home Guard and 50 officers and men from regular forces. Fire Guards demonstrated at Shire Hall with use of live incendiary bombs, phosphorus and smoke grenades – all very realistic.

Official Records of Bomb Damage in the Borough of Dorchester

3 September 1939 – 3 September 1941, 9 HE (exploded), 2 oil bombs (exploded) 1 oil bomb (unexploded) 10 UXBs, 200 incendiaries. No killed or injured. No planes crashed (English or German).

1 November 1941 – 31 August 1942 1 raid – 5 houses extremely damaged, 65 houses slightly damaged.

Summary

HEs   32
UXBs   16
IB   600 (approximately)
Oil   1

No Phos (UXB), parachute mines, magnetic mines or firepots.

Casualties   3 slightly injured
Buildings   254 damaged

In the Borough of Dorchester and the Dorchester Rural District Council area, there were a total of 784 'red' warnings, 464 purple messages, 1392 yellow messages (ceased 28 October 1941), 23 green messages and 2131 'white' messages

NINE

The War Continues

After the Battle of Britain, Dorchester settled down to getting on with the war. The town was packed with troops in preparation for an enemy landing, all of whom needed feeding. The following recreational facilities and canteens were set up all over Dorchester.

The YMCA, Icen Way. As early as September 1939 it was decided to send a letter to the military authorities offering to place the YMCA building at their disposal. It was already being used as a canteen for troops, but they were now offering full use of the snooker, billiards and table tennis tables and the rest and reading rooms. Amongst the many voluntary canteen helpers were the Misses Eve Davis, Audrey Lake, Audrey Charles, Elaine Taylor, Mary Martin, Mrs Emery and Mrs Slade. (The building was also later used as school class rooms, jumble sale and as an Ante-Natal Clinic.

TOC H Services Club. In the Town Hall above the Corn Exchange.

Old Soldiers' Home. In North Square and containing dormitories for overnight accommodation. From here, tea vans would be stocked and made ready for their journeys to troops stationed around the Dorchester area.

Methodist Church. The Sunday School room with entrance from Durngate Street was eventually open all day, including Sundays, as a canteen for the forces providing teas, coffee, sandwiches, cakes and light hot snacks etc, manned by volunteer church members. Although all the helpers were volunteers there was a strict overall control and young girls were only allowed into the main hall to collect used cups and plates provided they were accompanied by a male; otherwise their 'place' was in the kitchen doing the washing up!

Old soldiers who also knew it as The Soldiers Institute and The Durngate Club still remember the main hall being hung with flags from all the allied nations and there was a smaller room with a billiard table leading into another small writing room containing an upright (and tired!) piano, well-used and with many people singing along, often to the songs of Gracie Fields. In the main hall were rather battered leather armchairs and settees around the fire-place and there was a wireless on the mantlepiece, a table tennis table, and various tables and chairs for serving meals. Down the one side were trestle tables covered with white cloths. Sausage and mash cost 6d; eggs, chips and tea was probably the favourite meal and cocoa cost 2d a cup. Notepaper and envelopes were free. It was much frequented by the forces, many of whom slept on the floor.

Other canteens were the YMCA Services Institute in North Square with sleeping accommodation and 24 hour service, The Red Shield Club at the GWR station and the YWCA

Members of the Observer Corps in the rifle butts at Poundbury. The man in the centre was C. Foot and the photograph was presumably taken after the first consignment of American rifles were issued.

Hostel and Canteen for Women in High West Street. Also in St Peter's Church in High West Street.

Many were manned by members of the Womens Voluntary Service.

The Milk Bar. When war was declared, Dorchester had nothing like the coffee bars that later became so popular with the young – even if one did have to eke out the one cup to last all night!

So there was great excitement when the *Dorset Daily Echo*, in its edition of July 15 1940, included a full page article announcing 'Milk Bar opened in Dorchester'. The proprietor, Mr S.P. Shooter welcomed all 'in these War days to a refreshing drink or a tasty snack'. The Milk Bar was open from 9am and managed by Mrs E. Etheridge with six assistants. Naturally it was well patronised by all members of H M Services and Land Army girls, as well as by the locals, especially as it was located in South Street.

Mobile Canteens also appeared in the town, usually parked in North Square, manned by members of the WVS and other local volunteer organisations. In all, Dorset had 3 vehicles which in May 1945 were transferred to the government to help feed the civilian populations in liberated countries.

Also, often in North Square, was a mobile cinema.

Auxiliary Eating Houses were encouraged to be built by the government, and were later renamed British Kitchens and eventually British Restaurants. In Dorchester in 1942 the front part of Thurmans, Ironmongers, at 64 High West Street was requisitioned by the Ministry of Food to be used as such. Officially opened by Major Gwilym Lloyd-George when he was Parliamentary Secretary to the Ministry of Food, the restaurant was very successful and well patronised – perhaps not surprising when you could eat adequately without having to surrender precious food coupons and a 3 course meal was on offer for 9d. I still remember the one spoon, attached to the counter by a length of string!

On the extreme left in High West Street, behind the telephone kiosk, is Thurmans, Ironmongers. In 1942 the front of the shop was requisitioned by the Ministry of Food to become an Auxiliary Eating House. A three course meal could be bought for 9d.

It has been suggested that some patrons smuggled a few sugar lumps out to use in their own tea-cups! It remained open after the war, not closing until May 1950 when it was de-requisitioned.

Local Firms on War Work
Eddisons. In addition to their normal construction of steam engines, Eddisons also helped the war effort by manufacturing the steel rings on which tank gun turrets revolved and studs to bolt plates on trawlers to make their wheelhouses bullet proof. These were the days when Mr Percy Bolsom was foreman. In the early days of the war, when invasion seemed imminent, they cut-up lengths of railway line, welding part back on at an angle for insertion into holes in the road to act as tank and

A Civil Defence Gas Decontamination Squad during a Ministry of Food exercise in the Cattle Market in May 1943. After the exercise, samples of cheese were handed out to the spectators.

The group below is of some of those involved in the May 1943 exercise in the Cattle Market. On the left is Douglas Jackman, Controller of Dorchester ARP.

vehicle obstacles. A railway siding from the main Southern Railway Weymouth to Waterloo line came into the premises.

Lott and Walne. The company traditionally made and repaired farm machinery, but as well as boasting their own Home Guard company they helped the war effort by making cast-iron casings for hand grenades and thousands of 3" brass weights to be used as the ends of rifle pull-throughs. Helping in the machine shop on the forges with the making of the casings were tradesmen from the Royal Army Ordnance Corps. At the rear of the premises (where Olds garage is now situated) was an old railway engine shed used by the army to garage, service and repair Bren gun carriers.

Channons Garage in High East Street, Dorchester (now closed) made parts for the undercarriage of Lancaster bombers. In the First World War they had made munitions.

Tommy Adams. On his land in London Road were stored crashed aircraft and the local lads would search the site for small souvenirs. Lorries with long trailers, piled high with crashed aircraft, both British and German, used the Top O'Town car park as a temporary parking facility.

Tilley's Garage was used for the repair of Army vehicles.

Air Raid Precautions and Firefighting

By an order of 1941, it was required that the occupiers of business premises were to make arrangements for an adequate number of people to be always present in order to detect and combat fires caused by enemy action. Also voluntary street fire fighting parties were to be set up. Most premises had a minimum of 3 buckets of sand, a bucket of water, a stirrup pump, a long handled shovel to deal with incendiary bombs, and sometimes a long pole with a rubber flap on the end, such as you sometimes see at the entrance to heathlands or woods.

In August 1941 the title 'Street Fire Party' was changed to 'Fire Guard' and personnel were issued with an armlet and a most peculiar shaped helmet without a chin strap. Signs appeared on gates around the town stating 'Water', 'FG Assembly Post' or 'Stirrup-pump here'. The term 'Roof spotters' was used in a DCC directive of May 1943 when it instructed those in the 'Crows Nest' at the north end of the Shire Hall to take up their positions on receipt of the alarm from the telephone and not the sounding of the alert of the siren.

A corrugated iron building was erected in the Weymouth Avenue recreation ground in the far corner near 'Stinky Bridge' to provide training for fire fighters, and many still recall having to crawl through the smoke-filled building with a stirrup pump to extinguish the fire and crawl out the other side.

On September 19 1942 Dorchester men aged 18-60 and women aged 20-45 were called upon to register for compulsory fire watching. It is strange how one remembers the little things. In my case it was my father, on leaving the house for his fire watching duties, singing 'Little drops of water, little grains of sand, lots and lots of buckets, standing close at hand'. He sometimes also sang the second verse 'Yards and yards of hose-pipe,

ready in the hall. That's the stuff to give 'em, when incendiaries fall!'

This type of humour was very popular, especially in the early days of the war, even extending to the ARP, which some comedians said stood for Angling Round Pubs. Even Arthur Askey joined in by singing 'Big-helmet Askey they call me. Big-hearted Askey that's me. Now that they've made me a warden, I get my torch batteries free'. If I can remember correctly the second verse went, 'Once at the sound of a warning, a blonde cried 'Shelter me please'. Then said 'That isn't a rattle: blimey! Its your knocking knees'.

However, not everything was so light-hearted. At a council meeting in September 1943 Mr Douglas Jackman, Controller of Dorchester ARP said, 'I would welcome a little more interest from the council – you may get exemptions from fireguard orders but you don't get exemptions from German bombs'. To which Councillor J.H. Moore replied, 'Everyone in Dorchester knows that the fire guard business is almost a farce!' It was also reported that there were many 'fireguard shirkers' – many had still failed to register. At a meeting in the Corn Exchange in North Square in November 1943, Mr Douglas Jackman said the fire guards acted as the eyes and ears of the Fire Service.

Cost continued to be important despite there being a war going on. When Dorchester became part of No 7 Region of ARP Control in May 1940 it is recorded that the allowance to local authorities in respect of clerical assistance had been reviewed and sanction given to an increased allowance of £2 per week.

In 1941, the D.C.C. granted a request to use two rooms of Colliton House and a small kitchen to provide recreational and canteen facilities for the County Hall fire guards. The cost of £140 to equip them was faithfully recorded.

The Dorset County Council and the military did co-operate and in March 1942 the military gave permission for a reception camp to be set up in the south block of Shire Hall, for storage of Civil Defence uniforms and equipment.

In March 1943, it was decided that Civil Defence personnel enrolled in the Home Guard would wear Civil Defence uniforms with Home Guard

The 40th ATS Company attached to the Dorsetshire Regiment at the Barracks, Dorchester, in 1941 – including several Dorchester girls.

armbands whilst on Home Guard duty. In August there was an inspection of Civil Defence personnel in Dorchester followed by a United Church parade.

Various changes in locations and personnel in the ARP took place in 1941, when the following appointments as Head Warden were announced:
Bridport Road area, Mr Kibbey, HQ Sydney Arms
Victoria Park area, Mr Harding, HQ Herridges Yard.
Fordington, Mr Troughton, HQ Mill Street Mission.
Monmouth Road, Mr Bullock, HQ 'Duffryn', Herringston Road.
Centre of Town, Mr Longman, HQ Friary Press.

VAD/RED CROSS HUT
Just past the old gas works in Icen Way on the opposite side of the road was a corrugated iron hut used both by the Dorchester Red Cross and VAD for training purposes. At one time it was also used by the local WI.

AUXILIARY TERRITORIAL SERVICE
The formation of the Auxiliary Territorial Service in 1938 was followed by a call to 'action stations' in August 1939. When, in 1941, women were liable for military service, women from all walks of life rushed to join.

Units were often attached to a particular regular army regiment and one such, the 40th ATS Company was attached to the Dorsetshire Regiment in Dorchester. Their HQ was the barracks at the Top O'Town. Their accommodation included Dorford Baptist church and huts on Poundbury Camp. This ATS unit included several Dorchester girls, including Marcella Barton (later Marcella Perham), Diana Durden and Gladys Coltart and local girls were given a cash allowance if they lived at home. Their commanding officer was Lady Digby.

TEN

But Life Goes On

SHORTAGES

As the war dragged on, Dorchester residents gritted their teeth, drew their belts in and simply 'Got on with it'. Being an island and having to rely on imports being brought in by sea, there were, of course, many shortages covering a wide range of items.

The words 'in short supply' in a shop really meant out of stock and that the chances of getting any more were remote. Further questioning usually brought the stock reply, 'Don't you know there's a war on?' Traditional copper items became plastic. With munitions a priority, items such as saucepans and kettles became extremely scarce. I remember my father finding razor blades difficult to find, and eventually going back to using his 'cut-throat' razor.

One, perhaps surprising, shortage was crockery, especially cups. All kinds of drinking receptacles suddenly appeared in kitchens, from the inherited best tea set of grandma's to tin mugs. Eventually cups without handles appeared in Godwins and were quickly snapped up. Knives, forks and spoons were also scarce. I remember my mother frequently visiting Goulds looking for bed sheets and blankets, which like all linen became virtually impossible to find. Even hot water bottles could only be obtained with a doctor's prescription. Another item that became scarce was furniture due, of course to the ceasing of imported timber. Even Woods had to stock utility furniture. The lack of wood also affected the making of pencils and I still have some utility pencils of bare, unpainted wood.

Even beer became scarce, especially bottled. Bottles themselves were in short supply and there were many appeals by traders, especially the milk roundsmen.

One item that soon disappeared was the kirby grip, a curious device intended to keep hair in place. Incidentally, ladies paid, at the beginning of the war, 1/- for a hair cut, 2/6 for a shampoo and set and for permanent waving, on average £1. A further annoyance was the scarcity of cosmetics, and I remember my mother queuing outside Boots the Chemist for a few lipsticks that had suddenly appeared. Another shortage was silk stockings, which could best be overcome by using an eyeliner pencil to draw an imitation seam on the back of each leg.

One Dorchester shop advertised, 'No more ladders – we paint your stockings on your legs' in order to create the illusion of nylon where there was no nylon. Liquid silk stockings were sold in sachets and bottles in Boots the Chemist with the announcement 'Gives bare legs the elegance of sheer silk'. One bottle was said to give 24 applications.

One premises to keep open through the early years of the war was Perham Hairdresser in South Street, which finally closed in December 1942.

If all else failed good old gravy browning provided an adequate substitute. To illustrate just how scarce nylon stockings were, a pair auctioned during a 'Buy a Bomber' campaign fetched £18 – a lot of money in those days. Soap was rationed from February 1942 – 3ozs of toilet soap for 4 weeks. Women looked for dusters to make into skirts or blouses whilst army blankets were in demand for conversion into overcoats:

Shortages even extended to railway engines, especially from 1942 when there was the need to move large numbers of troops and quantities of military equipment from one area to another. As a teenage boy living in a house overlooking the Southern Railway, one of whose hobbies was 'train spotting', I was delighted by the completely new area that opened up following the arrival of American Army railway engines.

Woollen garments were unpicked and re-knitted and blackout curtains made into garments. Stationery only became scarce towards the end of the war, but the Post Office produce an envelope with no gum and economy labels were often stuck on used envelopes. Perhaps the most embarrassing shortage was toilet rolls – the subject even being raised in the House of Commons! One of my female relations was both shocked and annoyed at being asked by an attendant, 'Do you require paper?' when she visited a public toilet. Many substitutes were used.

Milk bottles were shaken vigorously to make butter.

Queues formed part of our daily life. Many were formed without some of those in the queue having any idea what they were queuing for, and only finding out when they reached the head of the queue! 'Queue-jumping' was frowned upon and many times I witnessed those guilty of it being forcibly manhandled to the end of the queue.

CLOTHING

Clothes rationing was introduced in June 1941, surprisingly not because supplies were scarce but because they were too plentiful. Rationing was one way to save factory space for more vital work and to release workers for the munitions industries.

The first issue of clothes rationing books contained 66 coupons, which provided for one complete outfit a year. As an example of what a coupon was worth, men required 16 and boys 11 to buy a mackintosh whilst women required 14 and girls 11. Other examples were 8 coupons for men's and ladies' nightshirts/pyjamas and 6 for boys and girls, 7 coupons for men's boots/shoes, 5 for ladies and 3 for boys and girls. Seven coupons were required for a skirt and 2 for a pair of stockings.

In 1942 the Civilian Clothing Order introduced Utility Clothes, identified by the sign CC41. Leading designers of the time such as Normal Hartnell and Hardy Amies provided designs for 4 specified basic outfits, giving everyone the chance to buy beautifully designed clothes. Even this brought about a wartime joke : 'Heard about the Utility woman? – she's single breasted.' As the war went on, the words Utility and Austerity became increasingly familiar.

MOTOR CARS

Fewer and fewer private cars appeared on Dorchester's roads. Petrol rationing was introduced three weeks after the outbreak of the war. Books were provided in 2 issues with the number of coupons depending on the horse power of the car – eg 4 gallons for a small car (eg Baby Austin) to 10 gallons for cars of 20hp or over. Each coupon was equal to 1 unit of petrol which at the time of issue related to 1 gallon. Motorists had to apply for their ration book at either Dorchester post office or at a local taxation office.

Wartime petrol, 'pool petrol', also introduced in September sold at 1/6 a gallon rising later to 1/8 and then to 2/1½. It was an offence to store petrol in containers, garages or sheds. Also in September, the Dorchester bakers issued a National Emergency Announcement stating that owing to petrol and labour restrictions, bread would only be delivered in the town on a Thursday. Local brewers Eldridge Pope & Co issued a similar announcement relating to beer, wines and spirits.

Supplementary petrol coupons were issued for extra domestic or business needs and motorists were officially advised that to make petrol go further, one should 'coast' with the car in neutral, whenever possible. To achieve the same purpose some Dorchester motorists added paraffin to their petrol. Petrol rationing finally ended in 1950.

But not all was 'doom and gloom'. We still had 2 cinemas, several places in which to dance, plenty of pubs to drink in and our sports facilities. The general feeling was, 'Let's have fun today, tomorrow we may be dead'.

CINEMAS

At the outbreak of the war the Home Office declared 'All cinemas, dance halls and places of public entertainment will be closed until further notice'. This included football matches and outdoor meetings and any event that brought large numbers of people together. However there was such an uproar from the general public that the decision was soon reversed, and the cinema enjoyed a boom not seen before the war or since.

In the war years, Dorchester was served by two cinemas, the Plaza in Trinity Street and the Palace in Durngate Street. Both remained open throughout the war, flashing messages onto the screen when the siren sounded. Hardly anyone ever left to seek an air–raid shelter.

At Christmas 1939 both cinemas gave free film shows for all Dorchester evacuee children and this practice continued and often small gifts were given. On the outbreak of war the Plaza was showing 'The Gang's all Here' with Jack Buchanan, and 'The Girl Downstairs', a romatic comedy with Franchot Tone, whilst the Palace had 'Off the Record' starring Joan Blondell and Pat O'Brien. These were the days when the film show, in addition to the main and second films also showed a cartoon, and the Pathé or Gaumont News (always well out of date!)

These, of course, were the days of 1/9d downstairs and 2/3d upstairs. If you were taking a young lady with you the trick was to get to know the usherettes who would ensure you got seats in the back row. If you were going to the Plaza and it was pay day then there was the rare luxury of visiting the restaurant before the film started. In the early war days the Plaza was also used for the annual Dorchester Grammar School speech day. Later it was used extensively by the military, especially the American Army who used it for lectures and briefings. On a Sunday in 1940, the film show started at 7 in the evening. Queues would form about 2 hours earlier (mainly soldiers) and the latest one could get in (even for the most expensive seats) was 15 minutes before the programme started.

The Palace was known locally as the 'Flea Pit'. The memories here are of the usherettes entering the cinema 3 times during each performance armed with brass sprays and spraying the audience with a most evil-smelling spray. At the time we all thought it was to kill the fleas but I have later learnt it was scent. Saturday morning films were 'Tom Mix', 'Rin Tin Tin' and 'Pearl White': tickets were 4d and 6d (pocket money normally between 2½d or 1/-). Later in the war years patriotic films were shown, 'Desert Fox' and 'Desert Rats' were two early ones I remember. Also 'Stage Door Canteen', 'This is the Army', 'In which we Serve' with Noel Coward, and 'Millions Like Us' with Patricia Roc.

In both cinemas refreshments were sold at the entrance, and the programme was preceded by local advertisements being flashed up on the screen whilst music was played. Sometimes a prankster would manage to get their hand in the beam of light and make a rabbit and other impressions with their fingers, on the screen. The National Anthem was played at the end of each performance and everyone without exception stood, that is all that had not already sneaked out beforehand!

DANCES

The main venue for dances during the war years was the Corn Exchange, and the two 'big' events were the Police Ball and the Hunt Ball. Many bands played there but *the* band was undoubtedly the Dorset Constabulary Police Band – a large band with a big band sound.

Another local band, smaller but very popular, was the Harry Crocker Band. Harry, who ran a tobacconist shop further down High East Street, played the drums and was not averse to advertising his telephone number – Dorchester 282 – by emblazoning it on the large drum. His brother Les played tenor sax and clarinet, 'Foss' Waite and Maurice Moores alternated on piano (Maurice also used to play the piano at the Palace

Harry Crocker and his Band. Harry played the drums, on which he emblazoned his phone number.

Cinema in the silent film days), Bob Marr (alto sax and clarinet), Jimmie Heritage (trumpet) and Max Perham (string bass). Other members included Reg Inkpen (drums) who also had his own band, Maurice Masters (baritone sax and clarinet), Gus Kahn (alto sax and clarinet), Jimmie Bellinger (trumpet), Peter Amey (piano), Harry Burney and Harry Stevens (both vocalists and accordionists). Many members of Harry Crocker's band played for other bands. Maurice Moores had his own band whilst Maurice Masters, Gus Kahn, Jimmie Bellinger, Harry Burney and Max Perham along with Joe Pittifer (drums) played as 'The New Rhythm Band'.

There were, of course, other bands that played from time to time: the Purbeck Big Band, the 7 piece Novelty Aces and the Shamrocks, the last two both from Dorchester. The Shamrocks had Freddie Kemp on drums, Mrs Mitchell on piano, Reg Inkpen and 2 accordionists. There was also an organ and drums band with Roy Kenway playing the organ and 'Whip' Warren on the drums. I believe they called themselves Roy K. And yet another band were the Missouri Aces with Lyndon Moore (guitar?) and Harry Attwell (piano). Another band that played regularly in Dorchester

was 'Chas Bell and his Hotshots' from Weymouth. They won a cup for the best 6 piece band at the Melody Maker West of England championships.

Other dance venues included the Drill Hall, Poundbury, where the music was usually provided by Army dance bands – a small section of the main band from the regiment stationed in or around Dorchester at the time. Twice weekly dances were held at the Liberal Hall, generally in aid of one or another charity. I can remember one being held to raise money to provide uniforms for the women of Dorchester St John's Ambulance Brigade. These dances attracted around 120 people each dance night and the men were mostly soldiers. The same girls would turn up week after week and usually arrive alone, whereas for the barracks dances they would arrive in pairs.

Smaller dances took place in the local church halls and places like the Moule Institute, often with music provided by records.

There were also non dance bands such as H.W. Perham Concert Orchestra and the Dorchester Orchestra that included two Dorchester Grammar School teachers, D.C. Whittaker (first violin) and B.C. Cruse (trumpet). Several local servicemen guested with the orchestra.

During the war there was a Services Club organised by Mr Alan Jeffery. He ran dances on Monday nights, all monies collected being given to the President of the Regimental Institute of the regiment stationed in the town at the time. Entrance fees were 9d for soldiers and 1/- for civilians. And it was the Dorchester Services Club who put on the first war time concert to entertain the troops. Organised by local photographer Leslie D. Frisby and the Dorchester YMCA Committee it was held at the Corn Exchange on an October evening in 1939. 700 'Tommies' were given free cigarettes and were entertained with dancing by Miss Phyllis Mills' troupe from the Casterbridge School of Dancing, ventriloquist Bill Crocker, card tricks by Mr Abbott, tap dancing by Marian Dunsford, Ivor Creech, light comedian and George Wright with his 'illuminated clubs'. Mrs Heritage sang popular songs of the day including 'Just a song at twilight' and the show ended with twenty minutes of community singing. Harry Crocker and his band supplied the music.

Several well known bands played at the Corn Exchange, especially in the early days of the war, and I well remember the standing ovations accorded to Nat Gonella when he fronted his dance band with his own special trumpet playing. Later, of course, several big name American army bands played at the Corn Exchange.

Very occasionally there were tea dances held in the Corn Exchange on Thursday afternoons. The Corn Exchange was also used for pantomimes and concerts, often for V for Victory and Wings for Victory weeks, and including such celebrities as Jack Warner and Beryl Ord. ENSA variety shows were also staged there.

Also popular were the 'Socials' put on by the various youth organisations, the Girls Training Corps (GTC) holding theirs at the Green School, the Sea Cadets at the Modern School and the Dorchester Grammar School Officer Training Corps at the Grammar School. The OTC even had their own dance band; 'Skinny' Skinner on piano, Ted Shellabear, violin and piano, Ian 'Digger' Digby, on alto sax and clarinet and Bernard 'Bunty' Watts on drums. Traditionally these 'Socials' always started with 'a general excuse-me quickstep', usually 'In the Mood' or 'The Darktown Strutters Ball'.

The Dorchester YMCA 'Socials' were slightly different as they included games, the favourite

Chas Bell and his Hot Shots frequently provided the music at Dorchester's wartime dances. Charles Bell played the drums. Quite a lot of members are missing from this photograph, which included Helen Hallet on vocals.

being the ever popular kissing game 'Bobby Bingo'. Equally popular were the 'smooch' dances, with all the lights switched off! To get everyone on the floor one of the early in the evening dances was the 'Paul Jones' – girls formed an inner circle and the boys an outer circle. When the music started the circles moved in opposite directions and when the music stopped you danced with whoever was opposite. The trick was to keep one's eye on the conductor to see when he was about to stop the music and then either quicken up or slow down in order to finish opposite the person you really wanted to dance with.

These were, of course, the days of strict tempo ballroom dancing (shades of Victor Sylvester!) with the quickstep (every dance started with one), the waltz (every dance finished with the last waltz – very often to the tune of 'Who's taking you home tonight?', and the slow foxtrot (more difficult to learn but one could always do a slow quickstep!). There were also the Latin-American dances – the tango (mostly for the show-offs who had been to dancing classes!), the rhumba, the samba and the paso doble.

Most wartime dances included a small selection of old time dances – the Veleta, St Bernard Waltz and the Gay Gordons. There were also novelty dances such as the Conga, which generally finished by leaving the dance hall, taking a couple of turns round the Town Pump and returning back onto the dance floor. Especially riotous on New Year's Eve. Other novelty dances were the 'Palais Glide', lines of dancers side by side with arms round each other's waists and the 'Hokey Cokey'. I also remember a short spell of 'Boomps-a-Daisy', a loud rowdy dance ending with bottoms being banged together. We also danced the ever popular 'Lambeth Walk' (Oi!).

Also popular was the 'Ladies Choice', which gave the girls a chance to ask the boys for a dance and give the boys a chance to find out which girls 'fancied' him! In those distant chivalrous days the man formally asked the lady to dance and after the dance it was his duty to escort her back to her seat. Today, partners generally seem to dance a couple of feet apart. It was quite different in the war years. Where else could a male stranger approach a female stranger and hold her really closely for 3 minutes? And then the lady even thanked the man for doing so!

Many of us, in wartime Dorchester, learnt to dance by going to the socials and simply getting on the floor with someone who could dance. In those days it seemed that girls could either dance the usual backward steps or 'take the lead' and the boy's part. Very often, through lack of boys who could dance, one would see two girls dancing together.

Of those of us who decided to 'learn properly' many went to Miss Esme Slay's ballroom dancing classes held at the rear of The Bridge Hotel in High East Street. Here we took our first tentative steps, some of us progressing on to win medals. My dancing partner in those days was Miss Barbara Fry and others who regularly attended were Mr 'Curly' Barnes and Miss Thelma Kinnersley and Mr Reggie Moors and Miss Margaret Haggar. Margaret eventually ended up by being Miss Slay's assistant.

On Saturday nights, the same venue was used to run small dances. Organised by the Boot family – he was a prison officer, the daughter was Diana and the son, Malcolm: they charged 1/- entrance fee and the music was provided by records. I remember Miss Jean West, Miss Jill Daubeney, Mr John Baker and Mr Bill Tadd and the Thomas sisters, Ann and Mollie.

If one wanted to dance during the day, it was necessary to visit nearby Weymouth. There was great rivalry between the two towns in those days with Dorchester folk remarking that the only good thing that ever came out of Weymouth was the road to Dorchester! At Weymouth, afternoon tea dances were held at the Regent Dance Hall and were free for those taking tea. Evening dances were held from 7 p.m. to 10 p.m. and the entrance fee was 1/-. Incidentally, when war broke out, Henry Hall and his orchestra were playing at the Weymouth Alexandra Gardens.

Of course, dancing as we knew it in Dorchester during the early war years was completely turned on its head in early 1942 when the 'Yanks' arrived in town! Up to then the only 'foreign' competition for we local lads was from the airmen from Poland, Rhodesia, Canada etc. stationed at Warmwell. The Corn Exchange, the venue up to then for so many of our dances, was taken over by the US Army as one of their PXs. Their dance evenings were for US troops only but open to any Dorchester female free of charge! Not only that, but free buses were provided on Sunday afternoons outside the Corn Exchange to bus the Dorchester girls out to one of the US army bases at Piddlehinton Camp as dance partners for the troops stationed there.

The 'Hokey Cokey' and the 'Lambeth Walk' suddenly became very 'old hat' compared to the exciting jive, jitterbug and Glen Miller big band style provided by the swing bands of the US Army.

PUBLIC HOUSES

In 1939, Dorchester was blessed with a lot of 'drinking holes'. Sadly, many have since disappeared – the Swan in King's Road, the Noah's Ark at the bottom of Fordington Hill, the Three Mariners in High East Street, the Exhibition in London Road, the Great Western near the old GWR station, the Old House at Home in Salisbury Street and The Antelope and the New Inn, both in South Street.

Many people living in Dorchester today would find it difficult to imagine that at the beginning of the war Fordington was a 'no go' area. The police went there in pairs and with a dog if one was available. With the arrival of so many troops in the town, trade increased dramatically and even the

Fordington pubs welcomed them.

The Royal Oak in High West Street was requisitioned by the military but almost next door was the Old Ship, always packed with personnel from the armed forces. It was very noisy and not many nights passed without a fight. In the early days of the war, fights were usually between British troops and those from allied nations, then between the Army, Navy and Air Force and failing that between regiments. Later with the arrival of the American troops, their military police seemed to be permanently camped inside the pub! Often there was a good-looking English sailor playing the piano, with his cap on the back of his head and pints of beer lined up on the piano. I later discovered he was Russ Conway who, after the war, appeared with the Billy Cotton Band Show.

The Swan was popular with the Americans, not only for the beer but for the local entertainment. Little Billy Benham, a midget and reputedly 'King of the Gypsies', did handstands on the bar counter and drank every pint put in front of him. The black American troops usually patronised The Old House at Home in Salisbury Street. When the 'Yanks' arrived, the locals were shocked to find that they poured whisky into their beer. But soon they were introduced to a mixture of beer and cider that had been allowed to mature over a number of years – the locals called them 'Block busters'.

One enterprising local landlord advertised the matured cider with a notice on his bar: 'Scrumpy – you buy the first pint, the remainder free of charge'. The American troops just could not believe their luck – free cider! There was great demand with many American soldiers calling from their tables for another pint after they had downed the first. The landlord called back 'come and get it' and then the problem started. After drinking cider, the mind may remain clear, but the feet do not function. I lost count of the number of GIs, who on trying to claim their free pint, simply slipped off their chairs and onto the floor!

SPORT

Sport also continued during the war and I remember Dorchester Town, who then played at the old football ground in Weymouth Avenue,

inviting 'guests' to play for them. These 'guests' were mostly from Scottish First Division clubs drawn from regiments stationed in or near the town. At least on one occasion the entire XI were made up from the Army. It is perhaps not surprising that the number of goals scored by the town in those early war years often reached double figures. Oh if that were so now! The first match played after war was declared was Dorchester against Blandford in the Dorset League, which I am delighted to record Dorchester won 8 – 2!

Rugby and cricket were also played. Dorchester Cricket Club played many of the local service sides during the early war years and some first class cricket was seen.

In the summer of 1943, the Borough Council voted to allow games to be played on Sundays during the summer months in the Borough Gardens and all Dorchester recreation grounds.

WHAT WE LISTENED TO ON THE WIRELESS

The day before war was declared in 1939 the BBC merged their national and regional services into the Home Service on 2 wavelengths, 391 and 449 metres, which broadcast from 7 a.m. until 12.15 p.m.. The broadcasts can only be described as 'depressing' – news, gramophone records, endless recitals on the BBC organ by Sandy MacPherson and recipes such as 'Making the most of your dried fruit'. In February 1940 an alternative service was introduced – the Forces programme.

Also on 2 September 1939 those few people in Dorchester who owned a television set lost their service and did not get it back until 1946.

To help sustain morale, ENSA (Entertainments National Service Association) and CEMA (Committee for the Encouragement of Music and the Arts) organised and broadcast lunchtime shows for war workers called 'Workers Playtime' and 'Music while you Work' during their shifts. Despite ENSA being dubbed 'Every Night Something Appens' or 'Every Night Something Awful', these broadcasts proved very popular and well known artists took part.

Another popular daytime broadcast was 'Housewives Choice', whilst in the evenings we all listened to ITMA (It's that man again) starring

Tommy Handley. This was British entertainment at its best, a slapstick comedy of 'English' types lampooning the enemy, often using misinformation from the Ministry of Aggravation and Mysteries. The original series had characters like Mrs Mopp whose catch-phrase was 'Can I do you now Sir', and Colonel Chinstrap, whose response was 'I don't mind if I do'.

A later series introduced Ali Oop, a saucy postcard vendor with the catch phrase 'I go . . . I come back', Sam Scram, an American who was always saying 'Boss, Boss, sumpin terrible happened', Lefty, a gambler who suffered badly with his 'noives' and brothers Claude and Cecil, 'After you Claude – no, after you Cecil'. Another of the show's catch phrases, and used by just about everyone when bidding goodbye, was 'Ta Ta for now', shortened to TTFN.

The British type of humour was captured by comedian Robb Wilton, whose opening remarks were always, 'The day war broke out,' followed by a long pause, 'My missus said to me. . .' another long pause, 'What are you going to do about it?' We all knew there was nothing he was going to do which made it all the more laughable!

Other popular war time radio programmes were 'Round the Horne', The Brains Trust, Bandwagon (with Arthur Askey and Richard 'stinker' Murdoch), later replaced by Garrison Theatre with Jack Warner (Yus and my 'bruvver' Sid) with his own catch phrase 'Mind my Bike' and his many conversations with 'his little girl', Joan.

The Nine o'Clock News in the evening was always preceded by the comforting chimes of Big Ben, whilst the newsreaders themselves became household names: Alvar Liddell, Stuart Hibbert, John Snagge and Bruce Belfrage.

THE SONGS

Music played a very important part in the lives of both those at home and the troops overseas during the war. It raised morale and took the mind off some of the hardships and worry.

Our songwriters never quite achieved the success of the patriotic songs from the First World War, such as 'Tipperary' and 'Pack up your troubles in your old kit bag'. The closest we came to their popularity were songs such as 'Kiss me

goodnight, sergeant-major' and, a reference to Adolf Hitler, 'Run rabbit, run'.

With snatched weekends and brief encounters and partings, some of the early wartime songs had separation as their theme: such songs as 'Wish me luck as you wish me goodbye', sung by the ever-popular Gracie Fields, and 'Yours', 'The White Cliffs of Dover', 'You'd be so nice to come home to', 'We'll meet again' sung by the Forces Sweetheart, Vera Lynn and 'Room Five Hundred and four' (banned by the BBC for being too suggestive) Later came 'That Lovely Weekend', 'Don't sit under the apple tree' (with anyone else but me), 'Every night about this time', 'Don't get around much anymore'. What memories these tunes evoke to those of us who spent our early war years in Dorchester, as not only were they played on the wireless but also at the local dances.

Other popular war-time songs were 'There'll always be an England', 'Praise the Lord and pass the ammunition', 'Silver wings in the moonlight', 'Coming in on a wing and a prayer', 'I left my heart at the stage door canteen', while the army had 'Bless them all' and 'Lily Marlene' (originally the song of Rommel's Afrika Corps, but adopted by Montgomery's Desert Rats).

'Tin Pan Alley' tunes included 'Dearly Beloved', 'Moonlight becomes you', 'That old Black Magic', 'This is a lovely way to spend an evening', 'Sentimental journey' (Doris Day), 'Aint misbehavin' (Fats Waller), 'The last time I saw Paris' (Dinah Shore), 'Paper Doll' (The Mills Bros'), and of course Bing Crosby's 'White Christmas'. Many tunes were sung with changed words, such as 'You are my sunshine, my double Woodbine, my box of matches, my Craven A' etc.

There were a glut of dance bands: Ambrose, Harry Leader, Harry Roy, Jack Payne, Henry Hall, Geraldo, Billy Ternant, Lou Preager, Ted Heath, Billy Cotton, Joe Loss (with his ever popular 'In the mood'), the BBC Dance Orchestra, and Victor Silvester (strict tempo).

Plus, of course, the American bands: Tommy Dorsey and his brother Jimmy, Benny Goodman, Harry James, Duke Ellington, Artie Show, Bert Kaempfert, Woody Herman, And the most famous of them all – the Glen Miller Band with such unforgettable tunes as 'String of Pearls', 'American

Patrol', 'Pennsylvania 6-5000', 'Chatanooga Choo Choo', 'St Louis Blues', 'Moonlight Serenade', 'Tuxedo Junction', 'Take the A train' and many many more.

And of course there was always Reginald Dixon and Sandy Macpherson on the BBC theatre organ!

All listed in the *Radio Times*, which cost 2d.

One programme most of us in Dorchester listened to with amused curiosity, despite it not being permitted, came from Germany and from the voice of English traitor William Joyce. Quickly dubbed 'Lord Haw Haw', the programme always started with 'Jairmany calling, Jairmany calling'. No one actually believed the propaganda he spilled out, and he did make one glaring error that lost him any credibility. He said that German airmen had bombed the town of Random, after apparently picking up an English report that said, without giving away the location, 'bombs were dropped at random'! During one of his broadcasts he said the town of Dorchester would never be bombed by the Germans as, during World War One, the residents had been kind to the German POW's imprisoned in and around the town. After the war he was hung, giving the Nazi salute at his trial when sentenced for treason.

NEWSPAPERS, PERIODICALS, MAGAZINES

Soon after the declaration of war, Dorchester newsagents announced that, owing to paper restrictions, they would be unable to supply their customers with newspapers, periodicals or magazines unless definite orders were placed in advance. Their slogan was 'Help us to help you'.

Probably the best remembered daily newspaper was *The Daily Mirror,* not because of its content but because it featured the unforgettable cartoon character, café owner Jane – the 'Strip Queen' with her little dachshund, Fritz. Nubile and always scantily clad she managed to lose at least some of her clothes in each episode but remained virtuous throughout the war.

Popular wartime magazines were *Punch* (1/-), *Picture Post* and *Illustrated* (both 3d), *Everybodys Weekly* (2d), a mass of women's magazines – *Womens Friend, Woman, Womans Weekly, Modern Woman* (7d), *Good*

Housekeeping (1/6), *Woman's Own* (3d) and *Woman and Home* (8d). The only men's magazine I can remember was *Men Only* issued monthly at 1/3d.

Childrens comics continued as pre-war but now featured the adventures of heroic square-jawed men in the armed forces. Amongst the many were *Triumph, Hotspur, Rover, Wizard, Adventure, The Rainbow* (*Tiger Tim's* weekly), *Meccano Magazine,* the *Beano, Radio Fun* and the *Magnet* all at 2d, together with *Champion* (3d) and *Boys Own* (6d). The *Magnet* ceased publication in July 1940 – a great loss for those who loved Mr Quelch, the boys of the Remove at Greyfriars School and especially the greedy Billy Bunter. Younger children were catered for by *Tiny Tots* (2d) and the *Girls Chrystal* (3d). Many issued 'annuals' and yes, I do still have several!

Books were plentiful during the war, many being read by candlelight which somehow seemed fitting at the time. Books could be hired from Dorchester's Boots the Chemist for 3d a week and there was always the Chain Library.

CHILDREN'S GAMES

The ever popular Ludo and Snakes and Ladders continued in their pre-war form but almost overnight war-related games appeared: The Siege, Convoy, Air Support, Bomber Command, River Plate, Chase the Enemy etc etc. Children's drawing and painting books also took on a wartime look, their peaceful pre-war houses and gardens replaced by war scenes.

Even jigsaw puzzles reflected the war, and Dorchester shops advertised 'Epochs of the War', 'Battle of the River Plate' and 'Hang out your washing on the Siegfried Line'.

For the older children special alphabet cards were on sale at Frenches in High West Street, entitled 'The Defence ABC'. They were popular at the time but I can only remember a few:

'A is for airman all ready to fly, with millions of pamphlets to drop from the sky.

D is for dug-out where grandpapa reads, while grandmama knits the socks that he needs.

L is for lancers, where men of all ranks, have given up horses and taken to tanks.

N is for the navy, whose power is immense, our

A Hurricane fighter in the Borough Gardens during a 'Wings for Victory Week' in September 1942.

Members of the 905 Dorchester Air Training Corps Squadron inspecting the Hurricane in the Borough Gardens. *Left to right* Messrs Kelly, Collins, Thomas, Sherry, Cheeseman and Hicks.

pride and our glory, our shield of defence.

U are the U-boats, who always attack, a ship when they know that it cannot hit back.'

ADVERTS, SLOGANS, APPEALS AND CAMPAIGNS

Perhaps it is hardly surprising that with rationing and shortages, the government, partly to get messages across to the public and partly to keep morale up, started to use special advertisements and slogans for their appeals and campaigns. As early as October 1939, appeals for allotments were made by the Ministry of Food with the slogan 'Dig for Victory', and later 'Lend a hand on the land'. Other slogans were 'Make do and mend', 'Don't you know there's a war on?', 'Lend, don't spend', 'A stitch in time saves coupons', and of course the

'Are we downhearted?' followed by a resounding 'No!' It was perhaps stretching patriotism a little far when one Dorchester shop advertised a selection of ladies underwear printed with the words 'Washing on the Siegfried Line' and 'England Expects!'

There were many campaigns, the majority of which were aimed at the housewife. Many appeals for salvage – 'The war is driving Hitler back, But here's one way to win it. Just give your salvage men the sack. And see there's plenty in it'. 'Don't Waste Water' and 'Put out your paper for Salvage' notices sprang up everywhere around Dorchester.

In August 1940, 'Up Housewives and at 'em' notices appeared in the town. The 'Saucepans into Spitfires' appeal for aluminium was probably the most successful of all the appeals. With the Battle of Britain taking place in the skies overhead it was easy to imagine our old saucepans actually had been used to make a Spitfire. I remember some enthusiastic housewives, intending to replace their saucepans with new ones, gave them all away only to later find there was a shortage in the Dorchester shops!

The Ministry of Food issued appeal after appeal. One early one, again aimed at the housewife read, 'Your Empties wanted – please bring back your empty cod liver oil and orange juice bottles when you come for a new supply', quickly followed by 'Bring us your empty jam jars – make sure of your jam ration by returning every empty now'.

In November 1940, the Ministry of Supply appealed for 125,000 pairs of binoculars from the general public: 'Our fighting forces need them – sell yours now'. Many Dorchester residents responded but mostly gave them rather than selling them.

Food obviously formed a large part of wartime daily life and each week the *Echo* contained a Ministry of Food 'Food Fact' giving hints and tips on using recipes. Potatoes were a staple of the diet, one slogan asking us to 'think of the potato – think of it as a weapon of war', which suggested to me that somehow we were supposed to repel the armed might of the German invaders by hurling spuds at them!

Although it was never rationed, coal was quite scarce during the war and several adverts appeared in the *Echo* during 1940, all issued by the Mines Department – 'Use coal carefully, be glad of any coal, don't worry about the kind, your merchant will supply the best he can'. Others were 'Lay one fire only – light it late – let it last', 'Never waste hot water, never use sooty pans, never force the boiler, mix fuels if necessary, stop draughts in rooms, breakfast in the kitchen, stocks must be conserved – sift your cinders – spare the poker, save coal'. We were also encouraged to 'Whenever possible, burn logs instead of coal'.

None of which stopped my mother not trusting the coalman. I was always positioned at the back door to count in the number of sacks delivered on the grounds that 'they will bring in one bag short if no-one is watching!'

Naturally we were all encouraged to save money to help the war effort and slogans such as 'Hit back with National Savings' appeared. From 1940 onwards there were the continual Dorchester Savings Weeks, usually launched with a march through the town by contingents of any army unit stationed locally, together with the Home Guard, WLA, Fire Brigade, Red Cross, St John Ambulance, Army, Navy and Air Force Cadets and the Scouts and Girl Guides, all led by a band. Barometers recording the target and the amount of money raised appeared at the Corn Exchange or Town Pump and there were concerts held in the Corn Exchange. The ones I can remember in Dorchester were War Weapons Week (from September 1940 – October 1941), Warships Week (October 1941 – March 1942), Wings for Victory Week (Spring 1942 – summer 1943), Salute the Soldier Week (March 1944) and Spitfire Week.

In a War Weapons Week in 1941 a caricature of Hitler was placed on the Town Pump with the words 'Take that grin off his face. Save all you can to beat that man'. At the same time Timothy Whites and Taylors placed a large poster in their window advertising the event and not wishing to miss any opportunities adding that 'Everything for the garden can be purchased in our store!'

During a Wings for Victory week in 1942 an RAF spokesman told us 'Give us the tools and we will finish the job' and opened a 'special exhibition' at Genges, who had offered their ground floor for the purpose. A target indicator was erected in the town centre and a Hurricane was placed on show in the Borough Gardens (*see photographs on opposite page*).

In March 1943 the Dorchester ARP Committee organised a concert in aid of HMS *Dorsetshire*. Music was supplied by Melville Christie and his orchestra and the show started with 'a brisk and snappy number' entitled 'Rise and Shine' followed by '3 Little Sisters' sung by 18 year old Eva Beynon. David Henri then sang 'The Aniversary Waltz' and joined by Eva both sang 'The Twilight Waltz'.

In March 1943, a variety concert was held in the Corn Exchange in aid of the Merchant Navy Comforts Service. The show opened with music by the local Harry Crocker band with Maurice Moores on piano, followed by the singing of a gypsy song by baritone George Gray. Then came songs by the Casterbridge Singers, followed by Lilian Pusey on piano. Henry Martyn cracked some jokes and then came a conjuring act by Sansum and Nahpoo (aided by Madam Woo) and

A 'Wings for Victory Week' hoarding on the Corn Exchange, July 1943.

the grande finale, consisting of 'a splendid tableau by members of First Aid Posts'.

In one of the Dorchester and District 'Wings for Victory Week' in 1943 a large hoarding was erected on the Corn Exchange featuring eight RAF aircraft flying over the countryside and underneath 'Our target £100,000 – Our Total to Date £'. The amount raised was £308,000. In at least one Spitfire week, whilst money was being raised in the grounds of Fordington House, a pilot friend of the owner of the property, flew over the house and 'waggled' his aircraft's wings.

'Salute the Soldier' week was held from June 5 1944 when the town was asked to raise a target of £200,000. During the week, whilst making the appeal, the Mayor mentioned D-Day which had taken place on the 6th June. To help raise funds, a cricket match was arranged to take place at the 'Rec' between local cricketers, amongst whom were 'Jingle' Stickland, Reg Inkpen and Jack Wilding, with Billie Bragg as one of the umpires. The Plaza cinema housed a concert featuring Heddle Nash, Isolbel Baille and Harry Hemsley. A placard in the entrance read 'Get your own back –

make your money fight in War Savings'. The Dorchester Gas Company in Cornhill gave over a window to display Regimental badges. Local drapers, Genges, donated their windows to display uniforms of the County Regiment together with a portrait of the Dorset Regiment's first VC and the famous 'Marabout' gun. Despite the many calls on our money, Dorchester gave generously on all occasions.

As mentioned previously, we all believed that the country was full of spies and Fifth Columnists, and the government conducted a permanent campaign regarding secrecy. The original series of posters were drawn by Fougasse, the well-known cartoonist for *Punch*, showing scenes beneath the caption 'You never know who's listening' – perhaps the best remembered shows two women sitting on a bus, obviously exchanging secrets, with Hitler and Goering sitting in the seat behind them. Slogans were 'Walls have ears', 'Keep it under your Hat' and 'Be like Dad, keep Mum' , and

A War Weapons Week Parade passing Shire Hall, High West Street, in 1943.

'Keep mum – she's not so dumb'. These were later replaced with the slogan 'Careless talk costs lives', often with a poster showing a glamorous lady reclining on a couch and standing behind a trio of uniformed men from each of the Services.

It is interesting to look back at some of the local Dorchester shop adverts and their wartime prices. Tilleys offered a new BSA motor bike for £37 plus tax of 22/6d. Mens' shirts from Baileys cost 2/11¾ each. Woolworths 3d and 6d store had nothing over 6d. Framptons offered the best raincoats at 42/-. At Christmas 1940 Eldridge Pope and Co offered OHB whisky at 15/6 per bottle, sherry and port at 4/3 per bottle and Huntsmans ales in 4 flagon crates at 6/4d.

The Antelope Hotel advertised bed and breakfast £2 2/- per week, full board pension £4 4s, lunch 3/-, dinner 3/6. Guests were offered notices which read 'If you wish to be called during an air raid, kindly hang this card on the handle outside your bedroom door'

Several 'characters' and their slogans or catch phrases became popular during the war. One was the 'Squander Bug', a devil like creature with a Hitler curl of hair over his forehead and German swastikas over its fat body, pointed ears, tail and thin feelers. Used by the National Savings organisation, the 'Squander Bug' encouraged people to spend their money on unnecessary items rather than saving it. Leaflets carried the advice 'Don't take the Squander Bug when you go shopping', often portrayed under a big boot with the slogan 'Squash him'.

ELEVEN

The 'Yanks' Arrive

By late 1943, the threat of a German invasion had passed but the people of Dorchester were faced with another – a 'friendly' invasion, this time by the United States Army.

September saw the arrival of the advance parties – the engineers, and labour corps, soldiers who would set up the camps. The first units I can remember in Dorchester were the 701st Ordnance Light Maintenance Company and the 1st Quartermasters Company, housed in part of the barracks and in Poundbury Camp, designated as area D7. For the first time we saw half-track vehicles, jeeps and DUCKWS. The town did not really see many American troops until November, following the arrival of combat soldiers who would lead the invasion on D-Day.

On November 8, Dorchester and the surrounding district welcomed soldiers of the US 1st Division (known as the 'Big Red One' or 'The Fighting First'), veterans of battles in North Africa and Sicily. They were given a civic reception and the streets were lined with curious onlookers. The first impression caused several surprises. Up to now Dorchester had been accustomed to British troops in drab battledress marching though the town, their heavy hob-nailed army boots resounding through the streets, often with the regimental band in the lead playing their regimental march, and occasionally accompanied by their regimental mascot, usually a goat or dog.

But now we saw columns of American soldiers, their ordinary infantry soldiers dressed in uniforms that were of better quality than our officers' uniforms, marching silently with their soft-soled combat boots. Perhaps 'marching' was not quite the correct term: it was more a sort of dancing gait to music that was certainly not martial music. Their mascot was a soldier referred to as a 'Jingle Johnny' who was wearing and carrying lots of bells.

At 1.30 p.m. some 1000 officers and men were welcomed by the Mayor and Corporation at the Plaza cinema, followed from 5 o'clock by a cinema show and then a cocktail reception. The local papers called it 'a great success'. Certainly many soldiers and quite a few aldermen had a 'hangover' the following morning and at the time it was said that this had been caused by the shortage of alcohol resulting in a 'punch', which as well as being served in tumblers had been 'spiced-up' by the addition of surgical spirit!

As well as setting up new camps and enlarging others, all buildings that had been requisitioned after Dunkirk were again requisitioned by the US forces. They occupied the barracks, a huge camp was built at Poundbury and Nissen huts, each with its tortoise stove, sprang up on any spare piece of ground.

How were they received by Dorchester folk? Like any sudden influx, such as the evacuees at the start of the war, the welcome was tempered by some uncertainty. There was some initial resentment, mainly due to their attitude of 'OK you guys, you can relax now, we're here to win the war for you', which appeared to ignore the fact that the British had stood alone against the Germans for several years. At the time I remember we likened the American servicemen to their jeeps; the ability to ride roughshod over everything, to make more noise than others of the same size and to be instantly recognised by its appearance.

There was also, of course, an element of envy. Their soldiers were better dressed than ours, they were better paid, rationing meant nothing and they had an abundance of food, cigarettes, chocolate and . . . nylon stockings! In fact they were 'overpaid, over-sexed and over here!' (Their reply was that we were 'underpaid, under-sexed and under Eisenhower).

Many US troops were welcomed into Dorchester homes and they were always generous with their gifts. They never arrived empty-handed and knowing that food was rationed usually produced, butter, sugar, cigarettes, and sweets for the children. We in turn were introduced to peanut butter, instant coffee, Coca Cola, canned tomato juice. Children quickly picked up the fact that all the troops seemed to carry around endless supplies of candy with them and the question 'Got any gum, chum?' was heard throughout the town. We learnt what SNAFU meant – 'situation normal, all fouled up', and some of us even learnt to play baseball and American football.

Many children collected the covers of US cigarette packets such as Camel and Lucky Strike and chewing gum wrappers and stuck them in folders. The principal shock for parents was seeing their children handling real guns. With no gun laws in America it was quite natural for the US troops to allow even young children to play with their guns.

They were very polite, addressing everyone as 'Sir' or 'Maam' with a language all their own. We soon got used to the sidewalk (pavement), truck (lorry), gas (petrol), candy (sweets), and even rubbers (contraceptives). It is hardly surprising that the gum-chewing, cigar-smoking GI, with his seemingly endless supply of scarce items together with his reputation as a 'Hollywood Hero', swept many Dorchester girls (and their mums!) off their feet. Initially any girl 'walking out' with a US soldier was treated almost as if she was fraternising with the enemy and a phrase often heard in Dorchester at the time was 'She's only as good as she ought to be'. One joke I heard in the Plume of Feathers, where my uncle Walter Scriven had once been the landlord, touched on the subject. A mother, on being told by her daughter that she was to go out with a US soldier, warned her about the perils of so doing. 'Don't worry mother,' the daughter replied, tapping her head with a finger and adding, 'I've got it up here'. To which her mother, wise in the ways of the world, replied, 'It doesn't matter where you've got it dear, those damn Yanks will find it!'

Left to right: John Hallet, John and Marion Tetsall and Raymond Howe on an American jeep in 1945. The jeep was parked in Charles Street, at the back of the Conservative Club – then frequented by American officers.

Many Dorchester girls married their American boyfriends. After the war they were shipped off to the USA as GI brides, some to find that their handsome soldier husband didn't look quite as glamorous in overalls and stetson and living in a ramshackle shack with the rest of a large family some 300 miles from the nearest homestead. Many returned to Dorchester, much disillusioned.

As more and more American troops arrived, additional accommodation was required. Hutted or tented camps sprang up in and around Dorchester. Poundbury Camp was enlarged and 12 new ones built, all designated with the letter 'D'. They were D1 Dewlish, D2 Lytchett Minster, D3 Yellowham, D4 Came House, D5 Broadmayne, D6 Piddlehinton, D7 Dorchester, D8 Downwood, D9 Bincombe, D10 Kingston Russell, D11

Four American captains at the enlarged tented camp at Poundbury. Note the slippers and dressing gown being worn by the captain on the right.

Winterborne Abbas, and D12 Bradford Down.

Divisional HQ was set up at Langton House to the east of Blandford. Regimental HQs were Parnham House near Beaminster (16 Infantry Regiment), Ilsington House, Puddletown (18 Infantry Regiment), and Binnegar House near Wareham (26 Infantry Regiment).

During the US troops stay there were visits from the Glenn Miller Band and the boxer Joe Louis. There were also frequent Dorchester visits from the supreme military commander General Eisenhower ('Ike') and General Montgomery. They gave 'whistle-stop' tour pep talks to the troops, often stopping for lunch at the Shire Hall. General Bradley was another visitor and non-military visitors include King George VI and Prime Minister Winston Churchill.

As the build up of troops leading up to D-Day continued every scrap of land not built over or used for vegetables was put to use. Latrines appeared without warning. One lady who lived in an end terrace house took a long time to discover why she continually saw a line of tin helmets appearing on the top of a high wall on the land next to her!

Places that I can recall housing US troops were the Old Rectory in West Mills Road and Phoenix Hotel yard. Other places were used for cooking and storage. There was a cookhouse in the yard of the Plume of Feathers, and I can still remember the aroma from freshly baked doughnuts – they were in the shape of a ring – the first I had ever seen.

A large bakery complete with eating facilities was built in the Eldridge Pope and Co brewery sports ground in Herringston Road (now houses and block of flats). The entrance was rebuilt and there were high locked doors guarded by black American soldiers. Another bakery/kitchen was in the small triangle of land formed inside Culliford, Prince of Wales and York roads. It was also used to store both petrol and ammunition.

After D-Day both this area and the Brewery Sports Ground were filled with coffins. They were under cover but quite visible when the wind lifted the plastic sheeting. Other coffins were stored in the large garden of a house in Herringston Road near the Maumbury Road railway bridge (now a children's school). All a grim reminder of what was to come.

Huge stocks of gasoline were stockpiled in 'jerry cans' and drums in and around Kingston Maurward. Another stockpile was in the corporation dump yard in London Road (still there, now a lay-by just past the turning to Slyers Lane). Like the stocks at Kingston Maurward, it was guarded by black American Labour Corps troops. Most of these stocks had arrived by rail to be off loaded at Dorchester's railway stations.

When the black American troops first arrived in Dorchester they were given the same welcome as white troops, there being no colour bar here. So it was quite a shock to find that the colour bar in America also reached over to their soldiers in the UK. The black soldiers had their own battalions and segregation existed – no black troops were allowed in for the dances held in the Corn Exchange for the white American troops and there were notices outside inviting certain US Army regiments only (and no black regiment was ever included). I well remember some 1000 Dorchester residents attending a concert of negro spiritual songs held in Holy Trinity Church. The singing was wonderful, something one never forgets.

There was quite a lot of trouble between the white and black American troops. Fights took place not only after 'closing time' but during the day as well. I remember one outside Charlie Worth's fish restaurant at the top of High West Street and another between the Phoenix Hotel (home to many black troops) and the White Hart Hotel, both in High East Street. The fight in High East Street was not simply a few soldiers squaring up to one another, but about 150 white and black soldiers viciously attacking each other. As the US Military Police HQ was where the old Singer Sewing Machine shop was in High West Street, the 'Snowdrops' (their nickname coming from the wearing of a white helmet, gloves and gaiters) were on hand to deal with the situation. I must say their military police did not mess about. Whilst a few of them covered the area with rifles, tommy guns and revolvers, the rest charged in with batons, felling anyone in their path – this despite many of the soldiers – especially the black ones – wielding knives.

After this mass brawl had been broken up, High East Street looked like a battlefield scene from a Hollywood film. The injured were taken away by military ambulances whilst the rest were bundled into army lorries and taken to detention centres for questioning.

Jeeps containing 'Snowdrops' were a common sight in Dorchester crawling continuously up and down the main streets. They had 2 large bell-tents erected as temporary HQ at the top of the Grove, near the Top O'Town roundabout where the entrance to the DCC buildings is now situated.

During the war, what is now the Top O'Town car park was the Borough of Dorchester depot containing a public air raid shelter and stocks of Joe Whitty's coal over in the corner near The Keep. There were also two rows of wooden garages

A group of American soldiers with Mrs Parsons and her son Alan at 5 Edward Road.

owned by Nappers. On one side of the yard was a row of thatched cottages and after the yard was taken over by the US army as a food store it was a common sight to see children from the cottages asking the troops for 'goodies'. In return for the traditional cups of tea and cakes the householders were given tins of fruit by the soldiers.

The Dorchester children were treated well by the Americans and at Christmas 1943, 435 of them were entertained by the US army in the Corn Exchange. The troops had gone to a lot of trouble, putting up decorations specially flown in from the USA. Many of the children were collected by jeep – what a start to a party!

There were so many units of the US army stationed in and around Dorchester that I cannot remember them all. Apart from the units of the 'Big Red One', I remember the 16th, 18th and 26th Infantry Regiments and the 701st Ordnance Light Maintenance Company (I believe many were billeted by St Peters Church). Their HQ was at Wadham House in High West Street and many used Dr Harvey's recreational room or patronised Sandy's fish and chip shop. There was also the 1st Quartermaster Company in the barracks at the Top O'Town, the 459th A.T.C. (29 Div) stationed in Queen's Avenue prior to D-Day with DUCKWS and 105's, and the 489th Ordnance Evacuation Unit (29 Div) in Coburg Road until D-Day.

The 204 A-A Artillery Automatic Weapons Battalion of the 118 AAA Group arrived in Dorchester in April 1944. B Battery was positioned at Poundbury Camp and armed with 40mm Bofors

An American anti-aircraft gun position on Poundbury, shortly before D-Day.

guns and multi-mounted quad .50 machine guns. They only fired once in anger. There were also many units of female soldiers – WAC's.

The troops set up their own American Red Cross (ARC) Club and Canteen in the Town Hall of the Corn Exchange (the British girls were expected to wash up!). There was also a mobile canteen in the form of a converted bus manned by four girls selling doughnuts and coffee (this was known locally as 'the Doughnut Dug-out'). Units of the ARC often visited the US troops in Dorchester putting on shows for them (I remember they always stayed at the Kings Arms Hotel).

The Yanks just about took over everything during their spell in Dorchester – including the girls. I still have a 'knuckle duster' scar below my left eye as a souvenir from when four American GIs 'offered' to take my girlfriend Margaret off me when we were walking past 'Frenches' in High East Street!

It is important to remember that the American forces only came to Dorchester as a prelude to the invasion of German occupied Europe, and the ultimate defeat of Nazi Germany. During their time here there was perhaps one date that was particularly poignant – April 27 1944. This was the day when most of the American soldiers stationed in the town left their camps and made their way to Weymouth and Portland to board landing ships. To them D-Day had come at last, little realising that this was merely an exercise. An exercise with tragic results. Unescorted, they made for Slapton Sands in Devon, which resembled the beaches they would eventually land on in Normandy. Attacked by German E-boats, 197 seamen and 441 American troops were lost. This dreadful episode was hushed up at the time and it is only quite recently that the full account of what happened has become common knowledge.

Very little remains today to remind us of their 'occupation'. Some children perhaps, wider roads than pre-war (most roads were widened by some 2 feet) a few chips and dents on public buildings (the poor old Town Pump was hit by vehicles on many occasions). On the outskirts of Dorchester, at Winterborne Monkton one can still see the remains of a water tank which tested the USA army vehicles to ensure they were waterproofed sufficiently to allow them to reach dry land from their landing craft.

There is, of course, a silent reminder – of all the US troops who came into our lives who were killed after they left Dorchester.

TWELVE

Preparations for D-Day

Everyone in Dorchester knew, from as far back as September 1943 when the US forces started to arrive, that an Allied invasion of German-held Europe was only a matter of time, but we did not know where or when.

As winter turned to spring, the gradual build up of troops, stores and equipment accelerated. On April 22 1944 both the Great Western Railway and Southern Railway stations were ordered to be 'kept clear'. All rail and road traffic became the responsibility of the military authorities in conjunction with the local police. Many roads were widened and to control the convoys likely to pass through the town a one way system was drawn up for use at the time of the invasion.

In Dorchester there was a one way system from the junction of Bridport and Damers roads down through Bridport Road, High West Street, High East Street, London Road to Grey's Bridge, along King's Road to Little Britain then up Fordington Hill, along South Walks Road and up both Great Western Road to the junction with Damers Road and Weymouth Avenue to the junction with Maumbury Road.

Also one way were Trinity Street from the Junction Hotel to High West Street (as it still is today) and the whole length of South Street from the Town Pump to the junction with South Walks and Prince of Wales Road. Two way traffic was allowed on Weymouth Avenue, Maumbury Road, Cornwall Road and across to Poundbury Road. Also Damers Road, Albert Road and The Grove. All the surrounding 'D' camps had one way systems linking them to Dorchester.

On May 12 authorisation was given for white lines to be painted on all roads that would be used 'for offensive operations' and on the 31st it was ordered that to maintain road communications special permits were to be issued to each member

An American transport captain with his driver, in Victoria Park. As D-Day approached, the town became clogged with military traffic and lines of tanks, half-tracks and lorries.

of Road Repair Parties. Vehicles had to display special 'EL' badges.

From as early as 1943 Dorset's coast inland to an approximate depth of 10 miles had been declared a Regulated Area (this of course included Dorchester), and access to certain places was restricted or barred. Entry into this Regulated Area was difficult and one was often stopped and identification sought.

As D-Day approached, these checks became more frequent and thorough – another indication that the big day was approaching. Suddenly both the Great Western Railway and Southern Railway stations were permanently manned by American Army Military Police as well as our local police. Anyone unable to satisfactorily account for their intended movements was immediately escorted to the ticket office and guarded until, not only had they been put on a return train, but the train had actually left the platform.

The direct railway lines from Dorchester were of paramount importance as they linked the town with both Weymouth and Portland, which were the main United States Army embarkation ports. Not only were these lines used to full capacity before and on D-Day, but extensively thereafter, latterly bringing back wounded and POW's.

The build up of troops, supplies and equipment continued throughout May. In the first few days of June convoy after convoy arrived in Dorchester, filling the town. Tanks, guns, half-tracks, DUCKWS and lorries packed every street, nose to tail. Some roads had camouflage netting stretched from side to side giving the appearance of a dark tunnel. I particularly remember the Bridport Road area being a massive vehicle park, Sherman tanks were all along Dagmar Road, half-tracks towing field guns along Monmouth Road. Every field and wood was packed with vehicles all draped with camouflage netting. Latrines and mobile kitchens appeared everywhere. Poundbury Camp resembled a huge high barbed wire city, and it was said at the time that this was not so much to keep outsiders from getting in but rather to prevent the inmates from getting out!

The troops were not allowed to leave their vehicles except to lie on the grass at the side of the road. It was now obvious that D-Day was imminent and that these troops would form the spearhead of the invasion. Despite food rationing, they were showered with food and drinks and given hot water for shaving. At night many soldiers lit fires and sang patriotic songs. It was a period of apprehension and heightened emotion, especially as we all sensed that for many, these would be the last songs they would sing.

There were refrigerated vans all along Queen's Avenue with their freezing systems stopping and restarting right through the night. Although vehicle waterproofing was still being carried out,

everything appeared well organised. As soon as one convoy had departed for Weymouth a platoon of black Labour Corps GIs would remove all cans and tins from the grass before the next convoy arrived. Despite the close parking of the military vehicles, car owners somehow managed to get their cars in and out of their drives.

Many walls and trees bordering Dorchester's streets still show soldiers' initials carved with their bayonets. Even buildings did not escape, and initials were carved on a wall of the Planning Dept of the West Dorset District Council in High West Street and also the Victoria Hotel in Dagmar Road.

As D-Day approached no-one was allowed to leave the town and letters posted in Dorchester were kept there and not delivered until after D-Day, for security reasons.

On June 5 all army camps were sealed and all troops were confined to their quarters. My parents had invited two GIs to supper and were surprised when, not only they did not turn up but that they had sent no message to say they would not be coming. The next day we knew why: they were on their way across the Channel to the hell that awaited them on Omaha Beach.

Another indication that D-Day was fast approaching was the activity in the skies above Dorchester. Bombers flew to and fro across the Channel, often far from the Normandy beaches, to fool the Germans. Fighters patrolled the coast to prevent a stray German plane spotting the build up of troops and ships.

One night, with the vehicles parked nose to tail in every street and alley, the air-raid siren sounded and aircraft were heard overhead. Hardly any of the American troops had heard sirens before and there was panic everywhere. Almost every towing vehicle had a machine gun mounted on it, and they simply 'opened up' with every available gun. Monmouth Road had half-track vehicles manned by black troops. Suddenly the whole sky was like a huge fireworks display, but much more deadly: as I said earlier, two British planes were shot down.

Long after the 'all clear' had sounded the panic continued. The black soldiers were seen wielding knives. Rumours were rife the next day, including one that hinted that a handful of the officers and

NCOs who had been giving their soldiers a 'hard time' had been found dead from knife wounds.

It was in the skies overhead that I first knew that the invasion was about to start. On the night of June 5 I was unable to sleep because of the oppressive heat. Just before midnight I saw Lancaster bombers flying over Dorchester towards the coast and in the early hours of June 6 I heard the roar of aircraft engines, far louder than I had ever heard them before. It was a bright starlit night, visibility was good so I had no difficulty seeing the aircraft, flying comparatively low. There were hundreds of them, many towing gliders and it took over 2 hours before the last ones disappeared from view. The aircraft were Halifax bombers, some towing the large Hamilton gliders which carried equipment, including tanks and Bren gun carriers, whilst others towed the lighter troop-carrying Horsa gliders. The aircraft were painted with black and white invasion stripes on the fuselage and wings and the gliders had 3 white bands painted on the rear of their fuselage only. They were piloted by members of the Glider Pilot Regiment and six of those gliders were carrying soldiers from the Oxfordshire and Buckinghamshire Light Infantry, part of the British 6th Airborne Division. They had taken off from nearby RAF Tarrant Rushton and although I knew this was the start of the long awaited invasion, I had no idea that their destination was two bridges over the River Orne whose capture was vital. They were the first troops to land on French soil on D-Day, and the first French family to be liberated lived in the now famous café beside Pegasus Bridge.

It was an unforgettable sight and one I shall never forget. It was only later I realised how fortunate I had been with my temporary insomnia, as the majority of the town slept through this armada of aircraft – many programmed to wake up only if the air-raid siren sounded!

Whilst this was happening in the skies above, on the ground the convoys of American troops and equipment moved off to Weymouth and Portland. Dorchester awoke to find all the US troops gone. It resembled a ghost town. The camps were deserted. Packs of dogs roamed over Poundbury Camp looking for food. Local residents found tins of food neatly stacked outside their gates as farewell offerings. Apart from their official rations food was forbidden to be taken on US vehicles.

Like everyone else in the country, Dorchester knew that the invasion had started when there was a brief announcement on the BBC 8 o'clock news. This was followed with an official statement at 9.32 a.m. when John Snagge announced that 'Early this morning the Allies began the assault on the north-western face of Hitler's European fortress'. In the evening, the King broadcast to the nation: 'Four years ago our Nation and Empire stood alone against an overwhelming enemy and with our backs to the wall. Tested as never before in our history, in God's providence we survived that test. After nearly 5 years of toil and suffering we must renew that crusading impulse on which we entered the war and met its darkest hours. At this historic moment, surely none of us is too busy, too young or too old, to play a part in the nation-wide night of prayer as the great crusade sets forth.'

Although the troops had deserted their camps, it did not, of course, mean the end of seeing other troops, vehicles and equipment. Seemingly endless convoys continued to pass through the town on their way to embarkation to back up the initial spearhead troops of the US 1st Infantry Division.

On D-Day + 1 we saw soldiers of the 2nd Infantry Division ('Second to None') drive through the town, later to be followed by the US 3rd, 4th, 9th and 11th Armoured Divisions (part of General Patton's 3rd Army) and also 32 and 33 Armoured Regiments, 23 Armoured Engineer Battalion, 54, 67 and 391 Armoured Field Artillery Battalions, 36 Armoured Infantry Regiment, 703 Tank Destroyer Battalion, 45 Armoured Medical Battalion and 83 Armoured Reconnaissance Battalion. The noise of these convoys was so deafening that many Dorchester schools allowed their pupils to watch them – teachers' voices were unable to be heard!

Weymouth Avenue bridge was a good vantage point, but it was not long after D-Day that we saw US Army Ambulances heading in the opposite direction, from Weymouth to the American Military Hospital at Warden Hill.

Convoys passed non-stop through the town day

Free French soldiers taking tea in the gardens of the Parsons house in Edward Road, July 1944. Although the soldiers are wearing American battledress, there is a Cross of Lorraine on the helmet of the one in the background.

and night for several weeks. It was later estimated that 149,000 vehicles travelled down Weymouth Avenue during D-Day and the few days following – with no damage to the road! Not all roads were so lucky. The asphalt in King's Road was badly churned up and many buildings and walls along the route received knocks.

The railways were also at full stretch during these eventful days and it was not long before we saw train after train on both the Great Western Railway and Southern Railway lines from Weymouth filled to capacity with German prisoners of war. Most trains passed through the station, although there was a POW camp in Bridport Road and working parties of German POW's in shabby uniforms and overalls were a common sight in Dorchester.

It was not only American troops that were in Dorchester prior to D-Day. There were also the Free French forces. In the war years, Manor Road only consisted of a few houses at the top of the road leading from South Court Avenue. The rest of the tree-lined route down to Herringston Road was nothing more than a dusty track with open fields either side. And it was here that the Free French parked their vehicles, all with the Cross of Lorraine painted on the side.

Although their soldiers had been provided with English phrase books, the difference in language prevented much conversation between the soldiers and local residents. A handful could speak some English and told several people they were heading for France, who in turn remarked that they must be looking forward to returning to their native land – to which the French soldiers replied that they had never been to France and that they all came from Corsica!

THIRTEEN

D-Day to Victory

After D-Day, Dorchester continued to welcome soldiers, but apart from a few temporary stays the majority simply passed through. In late July the county was removed from the schedule of protected areas by the Secretary of State for War, the first relaxation we had seen. Because of this, one popular song was played at all the local Dorchester dances, the dancers joining in by singing. The song was 'Don't fence me in' and it seemed to represent the 'fencing-in' we had all felt during the early days of the war.

Air-raid precautions still continued. Thankfully Dorchester saw no V1s (flying bombs) or V2s. We were informed that up to 29 February 1944 Dorchester had 784 air raid warnings, bombs had fallen on 10 occasions (32 HEs and 1 oil bomb) and in three attacks, approximately 400 incendiaries had fallen giving rise to 3 slight casualties. 245 houses had been damaged and repaired.

A Halifax bomber towing a Hamilton glider over Dorchester on September 17 1944. The soldiers on board of the 1st Airborne Division were bound for the ill-fated attempt to take and hold a bridge over the River Rhine at Arnhem. That so many survived is due in large measure to the gallantry of the 4th Battalion, the Dorset Regiment, who helped with the evacuation.

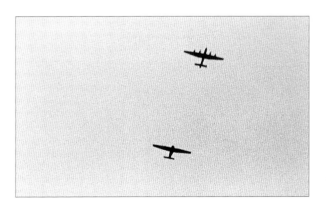

Southern Command of the British Army announced that all personnel in the Hampshire and Dorset District would in future wear a new 'flash' – the winged victory flash – to signify their part in launching the invasion armies into Normandy. The design chosen by Major General H.O. Curtis represented 'the launch of winged victory for Hampshire and Dorset'.

Dorchester witnessed yet another historic event on Sunday September 17 1944. In the skies above the town we saw 40 Halifax bombers towing 13 Hamilton and 27 Horsa gliders, having taken off from nearby RAF Tarrant Rushton. These carried soldiers of the British 1st Airborne Division on operation 'Market Garden'. Their target was Arnhem. A second air lift took place the following day.

From the intended purpose of shortening the war, the exercise was a failure – 'The Bridge too Far' of the film telling its story. But it will go down in history for the heroism shown by all those who took part. It was here that, on September 19, a Dorchester man, Captain Lionel Ernest Queripel, won a posthumous Victoria Cross for gallantry whilst serving with the 10th Battalion, The Parachute Regiment.

It was also at Arnhem that on the night of September 25 so many soldiers of the 4th Battalion The Dorsetshire Regiment (part of the 43rd (Wessex) Division) were killed and injured whilst crossing and recrossing the River Rhine in assault boats in order to evacuate men of the 1st Airborne Division and the Polish Parachute Brigade. Their bravery was of the highest order, carrying out a shuttle service across the river whilst under extremely heavy enemy fire. Several Dorchester men were lost in this gallant action. Amongst the injured was my cousin, Douglas Old, who before joining up had worked at Merchants

Garage in High West Street. He had his right arm blown off by mortar fire.

Many people had thought that following D-Day the war would soon be over. If anything the war ended more slowly than it had begun. By the autumn we were all fed up with all the rationing, shortages and privations.

Very gradually restrictions were relaxed. The hated 'blackout' was replaced by a 'dim-out' in September, and restrictions regarding car lights and street lights were also relaxed. All fire guard duties were relaxed in the town (as indeed in Dorset as a whole) and in February 1945 the Civil Defence organisation was drastically reduced in numbers. Buildings were handed back to their owners, cars on loan returned, and some ambulances made available for disposal. Civil Defence equipment was to be sold and rest centres closed.

FOURTEEN

VE Day
May 8th 1945

From the same room in 10 Downing Street that Prime Minister Neville Chamberlain had made his historic announcement that we were at war with Germany, the present Prime Minister, Winston Churchill, broadcast to the nation at 3 in the afternoon on Tuesday May 8 1945. 'Yesterday at 2.41 a.m., the representatives of the German High Command . . . signed the act of unconditional surrender of all German land, sea and airforces in Europe. Hostilities will end officially at one minute after midnight tonight . . . but in the interest of saving lives the 'cease fire' began yesterday to be sounded all along the front . . . the German war is therefore at an end. Long live the cause of freedom. God save the King.' This was followed by the National Anthem.

Everyone seemed hell bent on making a din. What few cars there were drove around South Street, Trinity Street, High West and High East Streets with horns blaring, the occupants leaning out of the window shouting at the top of their voices, many waving Union Jacks. Those on foot included servicemen and women, and all were shouting, cheering or singing. Around the Corn Exchange there was an impromptu linking up of arms, with some dancing the Palais Glide, others joining a seemingly endless line of dancers doing the Conga, whilst everyone else simply jigged up and down waving their arms in the air. Normally shy and reserved people embraced complete strangers! As usual the Town Pump bore plenty of young people who had climbed to the top. I remember one man banging on a large drum and another blowing a trumpet whilst others waved their football rattles. A makeshift 'band' with nothing more than pieces of wood and dustbin lids led the impromptu singing in the Borough Gardens. Everywhere was noise, but no-one cared – the war was over! Houses were bedecked with flags and bunting. Pictures of Winston Churchill, specially those showing him giving the 'V' for Victory sign, appeared in house and shop windows. Street parties, bonfires and church services in the evening were the order of the day. The last street parties had taken place in Dorchester in 1935 to celebrate the Silver Jubilee of King George V and Queen Mary – an orgy of lemonade and fairy cakes, then at the accession of Edward VIII and finally in 1937 for the crowning of George VI as King.

In Dorchester in 1945 the entire town seemed to be one large party with most streets holding their

Flags fly from a house in Monmouth Road, Dorchester, on VE Day, May 8 1945).

own special street parties. Trestle tables, wall-papering tables, and kitchen tables were all carried outside, together with an assortment of chairs and boxes to sit on. Tables were often covered with sheets of paper held down by drawing pins. Union Jack flags were draped everywhere and the whole atmosphere was one of a giant carnival – a celebration to end all celebrations – the war against Germany had finally come to an end. Although there was still the Japanese to defeat, our loved ones would soon be home, and we could once again get on with living our lives in the way we wanted to rather than how we had been ordered to. Freedom at last!

Food – even those items that had been severely rationed – suddenly appeared and was piled high on tables. And beer – whole crates appeared as if by magic. The fact that they were street parties – everyone knowing everyone else – made it an intimate occasion. Friends, neighbours, all those that had put up with so many privations – helping each other, consoling each other – could now all celebrate together. Certainly, I shall never forget that wonderful feeling of togetherness, that sense of achievement, of having won through, despite all that Hitler could throw at us.

Everyone was talking to everyone else, slapping each other on the back, linking arms and dancing in the streets. V signs were being made by young and old alike. The celebrations went on well into the night and the early hours of the next morning. Our Monmouth Road street party, combined with Culliford Road and York Terrace, was held in the open fields on the right hand side where the houses ended in Manor Road (then a dusty track). Someone let off Home Guard smoke canisters and some children became quite ill from the smoke. Dorchester children were catered for in the afternoon with impromptu fancy dress parades and children's tea parties – for once food was plentiful and many children were very sick! In the evening we danced the night away. We had done it, we had won the war!

FIFTEEN

VJ Day
August 15th 1945

After the ending of the war with Germany everything began to wind down and be disbanded and on May 11 1945 Dorchester gave its thanks to the Civil Defences. Later a group photograph was taken of those who had shouldered most of the responsibility for making certain the town came through the war relatively unscathed.

The Civil Defence 'Stand down' parade and Service took place in Dorchester on Sunday June 3. The parade was the responsibility of A. Hooper, Deputy Controller Dorchester Borough, assisted by Lieutenant Colonel P.K. Betty, S.J. Stevens and H.G. Read. Leaving the barrack at 14.30, after farewell messages from Douglas Jackman, Borough Controller, and Major C. Warrent, Dorset Rural District Controller, the salute was taken

The photograph of those responsible for Dorchester's Civil Defences during the war.
Back row, left to right: F.W. Kibbey (Head Warden A Zone), A.W. Jewell (Head Warden B Zone), W. Gardner (Report Centre), E.R. Bullock (Head Warden D Zone), W.T. Sansom (Rescue), C.L. Marsh (Head Warden C Zone).
Middle row: P. Thomas (Deputy Ambulance and Transport Officer), F.J. Derricott (Head Warden E Zone), C.W. Furse (Deputy Fire Guard Officer), H.C. Merchant (Deputy Head Warden B Zone), J.R. Walne (Deputy Head Warden D Zone), F.E. Jay (Rescue), H.G. Read (Training Officer).
Front row: S.J. Stevens (First Aid Party), J. Adrian Hands (Report Centre), Sister Marsh (First Aid Post), Douglas Jackman (ARP Controller), C.D. Hooper (Deputy Controller), Major R.G. Warren (Rural Controller), J.E. Skyrme (Ambulance & Transport Officer).

The Keep, Dorchester Barracks, shortly after the end of the war.

outside the Shire Hall followed by Divine Service at Holy Trinity Church at 15.15. The Service was conducted by the Reverend J.E. Gilbert, lessons were read by the Reverend H.E. Trask and D. Jackman and the address was given by the Venerable J.C. Chute, Archdeacon of Sherborne. The hymns were 'O God our help in ages past', 'Praise my Soul, the King of Heaven', 'City of God how broad and far' and 'Now thank we all our God'.

After VE day it was difficult to focus on the war in the Far East – apart from those of us who had relatives in the 14th Army (The Forgotten Army) and Japan seemed a long way away.

However we did not have long to wait. After the dropping of the atomic bombs on Japan in early August 1945, the Japanese asked for an armistice. On August 14 the new Prime Minister, Clement Atlee, broadcast to the nation: 'Japan has today surrendered. The last of our enemies is laid low. Here at home you have earned respite from the unceasing exertions which you have all borne without flinching or complaint for so many dark years . . . for the moment let us all relax and enjoy themselves in the knowledge of work well done . . . Peace has once again come to the world. Long live the King.'

It was perhaps not the inspirational speech we had become accustomed to from Sir Winston Churchill. Many of us were asleep at the time and did not hear the broadcast until it was repeated the next morning. The King spoke to the nation on the following evening, August 15 (VJ Day).

VJ Day was a public holiday and although there were similar celebrations to VE day they were far more subdued, less people turned up for the events and there was a general feeling that it had all been done just a few weeks ago. However the night in Dorchester ended with a blaze. Revellers took down the hoardings around the Corn Exchange and Town Pump and made an impromptu bonfire! I joined in whatever was going on in the town during the day but went to Weymouth in the evening to dance the night away at the pier bandstand, missed the last train home and walked back to Dorchester through Bincombe Tunnel along the railway line – to be honest I don't remember much of the walk, but obviously I must have made it home safely!

SIXTEEN

The Aftermath

After VJ day, further disbandments continued. The County Emergency Committee held its last meeting in the summer of 1946 with the General Purposes Committee taking over the responsibility for Civil Defence.

The reality of all that had happened came after VJ Day – restrictions, shortages and rationing were still with us, and it was not until 1954 that food rationing finally ended. Only then did one feel the war was really over. Although our world could never be the same again, we could at last try to get back to life in Dorchester as we knew it before the war.

The feelings of relief, of looking forward, were tempered by the realisation that the cost of victory had been high. 83 Dorchester men had been killed, many more had been wounded or imprisoned. The men, women and children of Dorchester were quite literally exhausted, both physically and mentally. But there was hope – hope for new beginning and for peace throughout the world.

I will leave you, dear reader, to decide whether those hopes have been achieved.

APPENDIX

Dorchester as it was in 1939

In 1939 the County town Dorchester was a municipal borough, small market town and the head of a petty sessional division with Councillor Charles Henry Stroud JP as its mayor, and Councillor William Henry Jewell as the deputy mayor. Market days were Wednesday and Saturday and early closing was a Thursday.

With a population of only about 10,000, Dorchester was much smaller than it is today. Homes in Herringston Road ended where it was met by Manor Road – there was then a small path through 'Stinky Bridge' to the Saw mills, then the Brewery sports ground and the Isolation Hospital. There were only a few houses in Manor Road from the South Court Avenue end terminating into a tree-lined dusty track, with open fields on both sides, before joining Herringston Road. There were open fields between Weymouth Avenue and Maiden Castle Road and there were no houses beyond Clarence Road.

The Victoria Park area was also much curtailed. Queen's Avenue only went as far as the 'Green School', Windsor Road was the last road before more open fields, and houses ended with Marie Road and Gloucester Road. In the Poundbury Road area there was of course the camp and Poundbury itself with houses only in the St Thomas Road, Prospect Terrace and Hawthorne Road square.

On the other side of town, housing ended at the Wareham Road end of Ackerman Road, and from the railway bridge above the top of Alington Road there were open fields on both sides of Wareham Road and the only houses were Max Gate and just opposite the entrance to Syward Road, a cottage.

Although it would surprise the young Dorchester people of today, when you were a 12-16 year old in the town during 1939/45 you kept very much to your own area – although naturally you all went down the town, to the cinema etc. and met in the Borough Gardens. If you lived say, in the Fordington area, unless you had a special purpose, e.g. to visit a relation, you very seldom went to the Victoria Park area.

In 1939, Dorchester was a bustling town well catered for by a variety of shops and businesses now, sadly, nearly all long since gone. The main shopping streets were as follows:

Starting from the North Square end, the first building in **Cornhill** (although technically in High West Street) was that occupied by Lloyds Bank – and one of the very few that remains, albeit larger, today.

In 1939 the manager was W.E. Brown, later succeeded by T.C. Buckingham, and it was the latter who was in charge when I joined as a very raw junior in 1944. Those were the days when on one's first day you were despatched to a shop at one end of the town to buy 'a hammer for striking a balance', only to be informed by the shopkeeper that they had just sold the last one in stock and being directed to a shop at the oposite end of town. And so on until you finally gave up and returned to the bank still clutching the unspent money in your hand! I well remember my first duty was to report to the manager's house at 8 o'clock each morning, light his fire and take his dog for a walk. Then into the bank to light the boiler and clean the inkwells. I cannot see many bank staff doing that these days!

Part of the Lloyds Bank building in Cornhill contained the stepped entrance to Thos Ensor & Son Auctioneers and Valuers, whose premises were above the bank. This section also housed the Dorset Horn and Sheep Breeders' Association. Next to the bank, at No 17 Cornhill and now part of Lloyds Bank, was a café (formerly confectioners Howes) run by Miss Ethel Major, who sold mouth-watering cakes. Then at No 16 came L.G. & W.

Morton Ltd, a boot and shoe store followed at No 15 by the Midland Bank, another building that has remained on site. Their manager at the time was T. Jeremy. Next to the bank, at 14 Cornhill, was The Antelope Hotel (now a shopping arcade), which proudly proclaimed itself to be 'one of the oldest and best known in the county'. The original early 19th century gates are still there.

At No 13 was the original small store of Boots the Chemists (Manager, T. Farlam) and at No 12, Braileys the drapers. This was owned by Ernest Brailey, who, like today's shops that advertise items ending in 99p rather than rounding up to the £1 above, placed 3/4d at the end of each item offered. In 1974, Boots enlarged its store by taking over Brailey's.

At No 11 Cornhill and 54 South Street (where Cornhill finished and **South Street** starts), was Boons Stores, grocers and wine merchants. What memories this store evokes – sawdust on the floors, chairs provided for customers and tins of biscuits piled up in front of the wooden counters. There was a distinctive aroma of coffee as one entered the shop, mingling with the smells of bacon – sliced as you waited, cheese – cut with a wire, and sugar – poured into blue bags, folded neatly at the top. Your hand-written shopping list was crossed off, item by item, in pencil, added up (no calculators then) and, along with your money, placed into a screw cup above head height and with a deft pull on a handle, sent along wires to the cashier's desk. The cashier, a most overworked individual – with screw cups arriving from all departments of the shop – would check the transaction and return the cup, with any change required, to its sender. In the meantime your purchases had been packed into a box and you left with 'Thank you, please call again' ringing in your ears. One other service Boons Stores provided was cycling out to the surrounding villages, collecting orders, with delivery next day guaranteed.

Between Lloyds Bank and Boons Stores were handcarts or barrows selling fruit and vegetables, perhaps a reminder of the old medieval market – one in particular I remember, run by, I believe, 'Sackie' Barrett and his wife. 'Sackie' was invariably dressed in brown overcoat, cap and muffler with a cigarette hanging from his lips,

leaving both hands free to serve customers.

Next to Boons Stores was the hardware store of Timothy Whites, formerly the site of the Post Office, followed at No 52a by The John Farmer Shoe Co, one of many in the town. At No 52 was the chemists, E.C. Clark, followed at No 51 by confectioners C.H. Stroud, where one could obtain refreshments after a long day of shopping. Number 50a Cornhill housed the county fruit and flowers supplier known locally as Rogers, not surprisingly as it was run by S.R. Rogers. It advertised 'Wreaths artistically arranged'.

At No 50 was the National Provincial Bank Ltd, managed by D.S. Carsons, a friendly, likeable man who, unlike most of his fellow bank managers, would actually talk to juniors like myself! The N.P. Chambers housed Sydney Jackson, Chartered Architect and Surveyor, and P. and J. Keniston, tailors, while next door – at No 49 – was another bank, The Westminster Bank Ltd, with F.D. Harper as manager. These two banks later amalgamated to become the present NatWest Bank in the former Westminster Bank premises. No 48b housed Goulds the drapers, with 48a occupied by E. & A. Shellabear, fancy drapers, wools and art needlework and the registered office for 'Servants'.

Two large stores followed – the perennially popular Marks and Spencer at No 48, where in 1939 an Ingersoll watch cost five shillings and, at No 47, F.W. Woolworth & Co with its red and gold decoration, lovely wooden floors and counters partitioned with glass into small sections with items costing but a few pence – hence its name, the 'threepenny and sixpenny' store. To overcome their proud boast that nothing in the store would cost more than 6d, one could buy a 2/6d item in five different parts costing 6d each!

One could smell the next shop well before one reached it – MacFisheries, a fresh fish shop managed by C. Annetts. I remember the end wall stuck out into the pavement, leaving very little space to pass. This was No 46a with, next door at No 46, Liptons Ltd, a provision shop managed by E.R. Hewer. No 45 housed the large premises of Tilleys Motor Showrooms, where the latest Austin cars were displayed for sale. I recall the entrance was in the middle, with large glass windows either side of it. At No 44 was The Central Temperance Hotel, known locally as 'Buglers' (A.T.H. Bugler, proprietor).

The existing General Post Office occupied No 43 South Street and in 1939 the Postmaster was F.J. Ewins. This was on the corner of New Street and the shop on the other side at No 41a was R.N. Dawes, a gentlemen's outfitters – 'Dorchester Grammar School Clothing always in stock'. The store was managed by Mr Karn. It was later Kitzerows shoe shop and it is now a card shop.

There was no number 42 and at No 41 was R.M. Dawes, who ran a Wireless and Electrical Engineers shop. Then came, at No 40a, Emery and Meech, Ladies and Children's Outfitters ('local agents for Chilprufe') and No 40, a hairdresser's and wig maker's managed by H.W. Perham.

R.J. Watts, 'Cycle specialists and Battery Station', was at No 39 and I recall this was where my mother took our wireless batteries to be charged. The premises also housed Petter and Warren, Chartered Architects and is now a café. Next came, at No 38, Matthews, booksellers and stationers (and official agents in Dorchester for Achille Serre). It also housed the Financial Insurance Co (Resident Inspector, J.E. Cox) and the Jill Scott Servants Registry, which is now occupied by Martins. At No 37 and now a jewellers was John Carter, Tobacconist and Confectioners, and also Cousins & Co., Turf Accountants.

Next came **South Terrace** with at No 6, Wilfred Snook, Radio and Furniture, and at No 5, J.M. Fry, the Dorsetshire Dairies. At No 4 was dentist R.A. Colmer. No 3 was Keeches, grocers who offered 'High class goods at competitive prices and where personal attention is assured'. The owner was R.W. Keech. The next two buildings were No 2, housing K.A. Holland, Accountant Rating and Valuation Office for the Borough of Dorchester, and at No 1, hairdressers, Popes, run by F.G. and G.A.S. Pope.

The premises numbers then switch back to **South Street** and at No 36 was A.E. Sams, 'boot repairers and dry cleaners' – also housing the Road Transport and General Insurance Company. Next, at No 35 was W. Hurdle, Butchers and Provision Merchants, well known for its tasty sausages.

Worlds Stores, until recently, Michael Dench, Carpets, occupied No 34 with, at No 33, Robert Davies Ltd, a mens' outfitters managed by H.F. Mitcham – where I purchased my first suit and trilby hat to enable me to be correctly dressed to work in Lloyds Bank where the senior staff wore bowler hats! A.E. Moore, Tobacconist and Confectioners, came next at No 33, followed at No 32 by W.C.L. Parsons, another tobacconist, and finally, at No 31, and coming around into Trinity Street, Tilleys, Motor Cycle and Cycle Engineers. The repair shop for bicycles could be found in Trinity Street and they also sold prams and toys. One model displayed by Tilleys in 1939 was a BSA 249cc Model C 10 motorcycle 'with electric lighting and horn' offered at £37 plus tax of 22 shillings and sixpence (22/6 as it was then written)!

Opposite Tilleys at the Cenotaph end of South Street was a large building that contained three shops. Partly in South Walks and at No 30 was James Foot Ltd, Corn, Cake, Coal and forage merchants, also selling pets and garden furniture. Their advertisements offered 'garden and lawn grass seeds a speciality. All your pet requirements.' My parents were never allowed to pass this shop without taking me in to look at the cages of puppies and kittens! H. Jameson was the manager. The other shops were, at No 29, Rogers, fruiterers and florists run by W. Ollerenshaw and No 28, W.G. Hyde, a small watch-making business owned by J. Clench. No 27 South Street was the New Inn, a public house now long since gone. A delightful building, much of it still there – the gabled windows, high chimneys and colourful green tiles, and also the old name and the E.P. logo, a reminder that it was an Eldridge Pope and Co. house.

The next building housed two premises – at No 26, now a travel agency, was the old *Dorset Daily Echo* and *Weymouth Despatch* office with a Mr A.R. Adlam in charge. At the time there was a young cub reporter, one Bill Tadd – wonder what happened to him? On Saturdays all the latest football results would be obtained from the pink (or was it green?) evening paper.

Next door at No 25 was a shoe shop, A. Jones and Sons, the building also housing A. Allen, rate collector and Frank Bertram, turf accountant. Then came – and still remains – the Congregational Church at No 24 South Street, at No 23a, the Fashion Shop with J. Powell as proprietor and at No 23, F. Gardiner, cooked meat specialists. These two premises later became a Grill Bar Restaurant and Shooters Bakery. How the memory plays tricks as I felt sure the Milk Bar was next to the Congregational Church – run by the Etheridge family (actually it opened in July 1940).

South Street Passage was and still is next followed at No 22 by Houghtons, the drapers owned by A.R. Houghton. I went to school with Ray Houghton who also, I believe, had a similar shop in Shaftesbury. They proudly advertised as 'Dorchester's most progressive department store'. Goulds now occupy the premises. The next three premises, R.A. Cottman, chemist and optician, at No 21a, The Cigar Box with Mrs D.R. Dean as proprietor at No 21 and the old Dorchester Grammar School building at No 20 were later demolished to make way for the present Hardye Arcade. Surely a more eye-pleasing replacement could have been found? The Charles Street entrance is particularly drab. In 1939 the old school buildings housed L.W. Beavis, optician, Pullars of Perth, cleaners and dyers, Hy Duke & Son, land agents, auctioneers and valuers, Thos Pearce and Clayton, chartered accountants, the registered offices of the Dorchester Building Society and the Weymouth Bathing Saloon Co., The Liverpool, London and Globe Insurance Agency (resident inspector J.E.A. Hammond) and H. Harding & Son, ladies and gents' tailors, 'specialities, hunting and riding breeches and liveries'.

Nappers Mite Almshouses came next at No 19 and in 1939 were the home of the Hand-in-Hand Lodge of Oddfellows Registered Office (H. Mills, secretary) and the British Legion County Office (secretary, Col. J.D. Belgrave), with a Miss Finch as caretaker. Then came, at No 18b, A.H. Scott & Son, fishmongers – I seem to remember a Reg Smith worked there. It pointed out to its customers that 'all the fish and poultry are displayed under hygienic conditions in covered and refrigerated serving counters'. At 18a was

Barrett & Son, decorators, and at No 18 was Elliotts Dairy, with Miss G.M. Palmer as proprietor.

At No 17 South Street were the old established ironmonger's firm of Thurman, who were the agents for Esse Cookers.

Until 1932 it looked like many other such stores in Dorchester – door in the centre, with large glass windows either side and living accommodation above. This gave way to a most striking design – large windows on three floors – the frames of stainless steel – as were the entrance and shop name. The roof tiles were blue glazed and the facings of the building was 'black faience relieved with blue'. Such a shame it was later pulled down and replaced with a new building housing Liptons. The proprietor in 1939 was J.E. Skyrme and in those days one could purchase a single nail, instead of the present day packets with more items than one wants.

Next to Thurman's (the locals always placed a 's' on the end of the name) at No 16 was F.J. Thornton, veterinary surgeon (later part of Tesco's). I seem to remember his surgery was in Durngate Street. There was also a Paul Thornton who was the veterinary surgeon to the Ministry of Agriculture. The Dorchester Conservative Club was next at No 15, stewarded by H. Partridge and often helped by his daughter, Eileen.

Situated almost opposite the Post Office is No 14, which remains much the same as it did 60 years ago. But whereas then it was the International Tea Stores, it is now a sports shop. At No 13 was G. Hepworth, tailors and outfitters, and this also housed the Refuge Assurance Co. Ltd, with G. Holmes as superintendent and Rendell & Co., Solicitors (also solicitors to the Dorchester & District Mutual Trade Society). This is now Next. At No 12 was Tizard & Son, tea and coffee merchants with their two very large, highly-coloured ceramic vases displayed in their window, followed, at No 11, by the solicitors, Symonds & Sons, which also housed the Justices Clerk's offices. The department store Goulds now occupies both shops. Barclays Bank is still at No 10 – and this is the building reputed to have been lived in by the Mayor of Casterbridge in Thomas Hardy's novel written in 1885. The manager in

1939 was T. Owen.

The next three buildings remain much as they were in 1939, except for the shop fronts. At No 9 was Sercombe and Hayes, furnishers and shipping agents, with C.W. Hayes as proprietor. Their slogan was 'Our business, your pleasure'. This is now Goulds. Still at No 8 is W.H. Smith & Son newsagents with P.C. A'Barrow in charge, while at No 7 was another shoe shop, J.A. Frisby. This is now Dixons. The solicitors Andrews Son & Huxtable were at No 6 – the building also contained the British Law Fire Insurance Co. Ltd the registered office of the Swanage Steam Laundry Co. Ltd, the registered office of Weymouth Steam Laundry, the local office of the Abbey Road Building Society, and E.J. Stevens, office of clerk to the commissioners of taxes for Dorchester and Cerne Divisions.

The next building, again much the same at the top of the building, was occupied by two firms, Lennards Ltd – yet another shoe shop at No 5, with H.J. Tarrant as Manager – while at No 4 was the Home and Colonial Stores. At 4a was the Eve Hairdressing Salon. My memory is not so good these days, but I believe the salon was managed by Sylvia Collins, who later became mayoress.

In 1939, on the site of the old Greyhound, were three shops – Floristine, florists with proprietor P.C. A'Barrow (presumably the same P.C. A'Barrow who managed W.H. Smith) at No 3, the chain library manageress Miss B. Treavis at No 2A (which was painted a rather ghastly blue colour, I seem to remember) and at No 2, Jewell & Norcombe, electrical engineers. Between No 3 and No 2A was a passageway leading to Greyhound Yard. Jewell & Norcombe advertised 'House, shop and office and farm installations, a speciality'. Certainly, if you were unable to find an electrical item anywhere else, you were almost sure to find it at Jewell & Norcombe! Each morning one would see Mr Norcombe cycling to work, usually accompanied by my father on his bicycle. All three buildings were rather shabby in 1939 and it was no loss (visually at least) when they were pulled down in the 1950s to make way for the present Tudor Arcade. Next came, at No 1, the Methodist church, pulled down in 1981 and rebuilt to house two shops, one partly in Durngate Street.

On the other side of this street at No 10 **Cornhill** was, until recently, F. Templeman, described in 1939 as 'saddler etc.', but who advertisted themselves as 'The shop noted for selling everything from a sack needle to a trunk'. Wonderful!

At 9A was the butchers, J.H. Dewhurst Ltd, and at No 9 Foster Bros, clothiers (L. Hern and A. Stone). At No 8 Cornhill was the furniture and carpet store Shepherd and Hedger (I went to school with John Hedger). The same site had previously been occupied by a store selling similar items under the name of Hannah & Holland. In 1939, No 7 was occupied by Jewellers, Tilley & Son. I believe an Eric Lyndon-Moore worked in, or managed, the shop. This is now H. Samuel, like No 8 selling the same items as the previous occupant. Another fine old building was occupied by three businesses – at No 6, the gas company's office and showroom. How nice it was to see items on display, discuss them and also pay one's gas bills. This also housed the office of the Sun Insurance Company, although the Woolwich Building Society now occupies the building. At No 5 was yet another shoe shop, Freeman, Hardy and Willis with F.C. Tomlinson as manager. The final shop, at No 4, was F.G. Longman, printer and stationer who advertised 'opposite the Town Pump – any book can be specially ordered if necessary'. They stocked all the books required by the Dorchester Grammar School and the premises is now occupied by the British Heart Foundation.

At No 3 Cornhill, now a building society, was hairdresser and tobacconist W.C.L. Parsons. The hairdressing salon was on the first floor and as a junior at Lloyds Bank opposite, I could wave across and I well remember one very pretty dark-haired girl blowing kisses back in return. Happy days! Although a non-smoker myself, I often accompanied my father into the shop where their shelves were always well-stocked with loose tobacco in jars and a good selection of pipes, many of which my father purchased. The aroma from the shop was very pleasing, even to someone who did not smoke. The shop had previously belonged to T. Pouncy, who also sold tobacco, and I remember the sign over the door was 'Parsons' and below 'late T. Pouncy'.

The next building, No 2, was Currys Ltd, sellers of cycles and radios. Doesn't it seem a long time ago that Curry's sold bicycles? This building is now occupied by a travel agents and a bookshop. The final building – at No 1 Cornhill – was, in 1939, A. Lewis & Co (Westminster) Ltd, tobacconists with A.W. Groom as manager. This was previously Riglar, also a seller of tobacco. The premises are now occupied by a goldsmith/silversmith and watchseller.

It is good to see so many of the fine buildings on this site of Cornhill in good condition and looking much as they did in 1939 – obviously accepting that the shop fronts have altered.

While describing the shops and buildings in Cornhill, it seems only right to mention the Town Pump, surely the most well-remembered Dorchester land mark? Built in 1784, it remains much the same today as it did some 220 years ago. Difficult as it may be to believe, traffic in 1939 was allowed in both directions. Later it became one way – from the Town Pump to Tilleys with parking allowed on one side only on alternative days – signs were altered each day to indicate which side should be used.

High East Street. Once the main shopping street of Dorchester, by 1939 most of the main shops were in South Street. However, it is good to see that many of the fine old buildings remain much as they were when they were first built.

Starting from the old Town Pump the first building is the Town Hall and Corn Exchange – as it was in 1939, with J. Rippen as caretaker. It was built in 1848 with the clock tower added in 1864. Because of its apparent lack of support this was known locally as Galpins Folly (after the man largely connected with it). It is said many Dorchester folk were convinced it would soon fall down but Mr Galpin must be laughing somewhere as it is still there some 140 years on!

Next door to the Corn Exchange at Nos 28 and 29 High East Street was the outfitters, Jackmans, who advertised as 'Next door to the Corn Exchange – men and boys outfitters for 50 years'. They also ran a series of 'adverts' based on English Nursery Rhymes, such as: 'Little Jack Horner sat in a corner, to fit on a new suit of clothes, it was pretty and neat, and it fitted a treat, from his shoulders, down to his toes.' This must have been a success because others followed: 'Hey diddle diddle, play this tune on a fiddle, let the people all join in the song, to Jackmans for boots, hats, home of good suits, what a happy and good working throng.' Not to mention: 'Old Mother Hubbard went to Jackmans cupboard, to buy her dear laddie new suits. She dressed him with care, for her child was bare, then she felted his feet with new boots.' And not forgetting: 'Little Boy Blue, let your horn blow aloud, to High East Street, bring a cash-spending crowd. A visit to Jackmans, Boy Blue please arrange, to provide your outfit, next to the Corn Exchange.' Jackmans prospered, so it just goes to show that it pays to advertise.

Next was No 28a, which was the home of The England Folk Dance and Song Society, Dorset Branch, Dorset Press Services Office and J.H. Miller, Chiropodist. Then, at No 30 with Mr and Mrs F.W. Bennett as manager and manageress, was The Kings Arms Hotel – 'The County Hotel' according to its 1939 advertisement. Apart from a section of the building until recently occupied by The Dorset Blind Centre, one feels that one is looking at the building very much as it was in 1939.

The next building housed two premises, the old established grocers, Ernest Parsons at No 31 and the unoccupied No 32, now a kebab and pizza shop and a Chinese takeaway. Parsons proudly proclaimed themselves as 'the food specialists' and 'Parsons Challenge Cup tea, specially blended in Dorchester for the water of the district', but it was their coffee that I remember them for. Their coffee-making machine occupied one window and even after over 60 years I can still remember the wonderful aroma of freshly ground coffee – not only from within the shop, but wafting out and along High East Street. Like all grocers' shops at the time, deliveries were made and I recall one of the delivery boys, complete with bicycle and baskets, was Ken Gillingham. I always found it very amusing that one of Parsons' delivery vehicles had as its registration number T42 (Tea, for Two).

Next door at No 33 was drapers J.H. Gillingham, managed by a relative of Ken's, Daphne Gillingham. The corner shop bordered

Friary Lane and on the other side, at No 34, was the large building of the Dorset Farmers Ltd with K. Weller as general manager. Woods 'house furnishers', were next at No 35 who also claimed 'funeral furnished and conducted crematories – at your service, day and night'. They had a simple telephone number in 1939 – Dorchester 66. Woods now occupy Nos 34 and 35. Goldies', as it was known locally came next, and at No 36 and were 'agents for Huntsman Ales and spirits' and there is little difference in its outward appearance today from that of 1939, with Borough Arms still painted on its façade. The next building contained businesses – chemist T. Cottman and Leslie D. Frisby, photographer, both listed under No 37 and W.H. Davis, grocer at No 38. Blandford & Webb Ltd, corn and seed merchants, were at No 39 and H.C. Bailey, tailoring and clothing stores, followed at No 40 – 'lounge suits to measure, a speciality'. After passing an examination to go to the Grammar School (one had to pay in 1939), I was 'kitted out' with all the items of clothing required, at Baileys' – among them two football shirts, one white and the other with blue and black squares, school cap, tie and blazer and short trousers. The building is now Magna Housing.

At No 41 was the Three Mariners public house, with mine host, S.W. Page. This was a Devenish house and the property is at present converted into residential use, but the old inn sign still remains as well as the painted sign, 'pale ale brewers', over the archway at the side of the building. At No 42 was drapers Goulds, followed at No 43 by Miss E.K. Gillingham, confectioner and tobacconist. This shop holds particular memories for me, not only because it was run by my late wife's aunt but because when I was helping with the stocktaking I came across, on one of the shelves, a well-known breakfast cereal with a competition five years out of date! Obviously well before 'best sold by and a date' was introduced. This building also housed the receiving office of The South Dorset Steam Laundries Ltd, which proudly advertised 'latest machinery and no chemicals used' and 'free collection and deliveries on receipt of a post card'.

Before the entrance to Greening's Court, at No 44, was E.J. Vaux, confectioner, and, after the entrance at No 45, G. Frampton, outfitters, who advertised as 'sole agent for Nicholson Raincoats – unquestionably the finest value in its price class at 42/-'. Davis and Son, cabinet makers, were at No 46 with next door, at No 47, the Chequers Hotel with C.R. Cruttanden in charge – another Devenish house. This hotel holds fond memories for me – not only for the drinks but because of many games of table-tennis in a room above the bar. The names of my opponents come flooding back – Jack Rogers, his brother Dick, 'Maxee' Davies, Bill Davies, Bert Jewell, Megan Seaton, Mary Bragg, Joy Whittaker, Beryl Angel, to name but a few. At No 48 was Wood's domestic store with, at No 49, The Casterbridge Hotel with I. and F. Turner as proprietors. One of the few business still the same over 60 years later as is the next one, at No 50, Isobel, ladies' hairdressing saloon. In 1939 the lady in charge was a Mrs Johnson. At No 50a was the Wool Shop, run by the Misses Russen and at No 51, another tobacconist, P. Hartley. At 51a was R.F. Swyre, butchers and at No 52, the Bridge Commercial Hotel with H. Jeffery as proprietor.

The last building in High East Street was the White Hart Hotel, another Devenish house. In 1939, Keith Reginald Pilley was the landlord, but my memories come from the time my uncle was 'mine host' – 'Bert' Harris and his wife, Nance. I was too young at the time to sample the ales, but remember spending hours leaning over the wall and 'fishing' with string and a jamjar. However, one bad memory is looking over the wall and seeing a drowned black and white dog on the riverbed – I can still see every detail after all these years. The Hotel featured in Thomas Hardy's *Far from the Madding Crowd* and it was from the bar that his character, Troy, drank and smoked. This was also where Gertrude stayed in *The Withered Arm* and the Hotel also featured in *A Changed Man* and *A Few Trusted Characters*. After the White Hart, which still looks much the same today, was Swan Bridge and London Road.

Just across the road from the end of High East Street another well-known Dorchester 'drinking house' and now long gone, was at No 3 High East Street, Fordington, the Noah's Ark Inn. In 1939, the landlord was George Ernest Legg.

Opposite the White Hart Hotel and partly in Salisbury Street, was – as in 1939 – fruiterers and confectioners at No 1, R. Palmer. The building also housed Peter Mosson and Co. Turf Accountants. No 2 was a private residence (occupied by J. Baker) and at No 3 was Clinton Ben Grassby, Monumental Masons. A.P. Shaw, leather merchant was at No 4 (now a printers) and P.H. Dyer, Grocer & Provisions – 'established over 50 years' at No 5. Next, at No 6, and still there until quite recently, was E. Channon & Sons, the motor garage, then with F.J. Bowering in charge. They then proudly proclaimed that they were 'agents for Morris & Wolseley cars since 1913'. At No 7, and now selling antiques, was F.W. Wall & Son, fishmongers with, at 7A, J.W. Herritage, cooked meats. Alington Dairy and J.C. Estwell bootmaker were at No 8 with Humphries, bakers, confectioners and caterers (Herbert Arthur Humphries) at No 9. There was also a restaurant and it was difficult to pass the shop without stopping off to buy and eat their delicious cakes and chocolates. I can still remember the aroma of freshly baked bread – our choice was 'a crusty tin loaf'.

Moving up High East Street in 1939 we would have found another nurseryman, florist and greengrocers – Rogers & Son, at No 10. Their nursery was in London Road and customers were informed that they could have 'price lists on application'. At 10A was W. & H. Crocker, hairdresser and tobacconist, which is now run by Harry's son under the name Phillipe Hair Gallery, and at No 11 was W.R. Fletcher Ltd, butchers. On the corner with Icen Way, at No 12, was the Singer's sewing machine depot, which was run by M. Thomas.

The first shop on the other side of Icen Way and No 13 High East Street was drapers H.J. Gould, followed at No 14 by butchers J.C. Hodder. Some yellow tiles at the front of the building still remain. Next, at No 15, was J.T. Virgin, confectioners and bakers. Old pictures show the windows advertising Cadburys chocolates and proudly stating 'Hovis bread as supplied to HM the King'. The building was, until recently, occupied by Guardian Newspapers. It is pleasing to see that the old yellow/green/blue tiles along the front of the

building have been retained – a fine reminder of the old 'Virgins'. At No 16 was the Phoenix Hotel, proprietor G.F. Paget, who advertised 'Groves' celebrated ales and stouts' and offered 'every accommodation for tourists'. Sadly, it is long since gone. At the side of the hotel was an arch leading into the hotel yard. This arch has gone and the space is now occupied by a launderette.

At No 17 and 18 was E.W. French, booksellers and stationers, managed by J.E. Lindsay. This was a wonderful shop selling almost everything connected with their trade. In my pre-school days, my mother always bought me, each time we went into the shop, transfers that I stuck in albums – and, yes, I do still have them today! Another well-know grocery store, G. Wright & Son, was at No 19, followed at No 20 by Napper & Sons, motor and cycle engineers. Run by E. Napper, they offered 'private lock-up garages from 2/6d per week'. They also had premises in High West Street. Next came the London Central Meat Company Ltd at No 21 with W.J. Goddard residing at No 21A.

Then came Church Street and All Saints Church with the Rev. Canon Harry Bowers, and the – perhaps ironically – next door at No 22, the wine merchants, J.F. Hodges & Sons. This building also housed Edwards & Edwards, incorporated accountants, as well as the offices of the Dorset Friendly Society, Dorset Rural Insurance Society, the Borough Treasurer and Accountant, Dorchester Steam Laundry Co. Ltd, Dorchester Local Savings Committee, Mill Street Housing Society Ltd, and Public Medical Services of Dorset and Dorset Insurance Committee – all with caretaker R. Gomer.

Next door was printers and stationers Henry Ling Ltd. This was at No 23 and the frontage is almost exactly the same today as it was in 1939, although now occupied by a travel agency. Ling's were stockists for Ordnance Survey maps and advertised that they were 'specialists in envelopes for all purposes and keep a stock of nearly one million at a time'. Very impressive! Also in the building was S. Duffet Estate Agent, the Norwich Union Fire Insurance Office – resident inspector G.A. Fuller and the Southern Counties Car Finance Corporation with W.H. Miller as the District Representative. Moving up to Cornhill, at

No 24 was the Dorset County Stores with their slogan 'At your Service'. At No 25 was C. Jeffery & Son, Gun Makers and Fishing Tackle manufacturers. The last buildings were, at No 26, T. Braybrooke, Jewellers, and finally, at No 27, Lewis & Co., Tobacconists.

My lasting impression of High East Street was the number of shops with colourful blinds and awnings.

Starting at Cornhill, No 1 **High West Street** was Lloyds Bank, which has already been discussed. The Bank house at No 2 was occupied in 1939 by A.V. Rixson. No 3 housed the Dorset County Club with R.G. Shipton as steward. Nos 4 and 5 housed both the Dorset County Library HQ (open Wednesday 10am-1pm and 2-5pm and Saturdays 10am–1pm) and the Dorset County Council Taxation Department (issue of licences 9.30am-1pm, 2-4pm and Saturdays 7.30am-noon). The historic Judge Jeffreys' lodgings was at No 6, with Mr and Mrs A.M. Willats as proprietors. Besides being a restaurant 'with seating capacity for 120' and 'tennis, cocktail parties and receptions catered for', they also sold antiques, furniture, china and glass. Next came No 7 – 'Ney' Gowns Millinery etc, manager F. Fitzgerald, and then at No 8 – A. Wiles, Confectioner and Tobacconist. No 9 housed the Halfords Cycle Co with a Mrs Roper residing at No 9A. J.T. Godwin – listed as 'China warehouse' was at No 10 and also extended into Trinity Street (now a restaurant). Their shop was always packed with china items, so much so, that one was always afraid of knocking something off the shelf. As well as stockists for Copeland, Dalton, Minton and Worcester, they also sold cheaper items right down to garden flowerpots.

Across the road at Nos 11 & 12 High West Street, were the large Drapers and Outfitters, Genge & Co. With entrances on the corner of High West Street and Trinity Street and the corner of Trinity Street and Princes Street, this was probably Dorchester's largest store in 1939. Their advertisement in that year was a simple one: 'general drapers, tailors, outfitters and complete house furnishers'. Certainly they sold quality items, and I bought several suits there. I am told that the store was run in the manner of the TV series 'Are You Being Served', with the staff lined up before opening to be inspected, to ensure they were properly dressed and with their fingernails clean. My cousin, Eileen Old, worked there as a sales assistant. Although this store has long since gone the name Genge can still be seen above the old entrance.

Moving up High West Street were several long-established and well remembered shops. At No 13 was a ladies and gentlemen's hairdressers, W.G. Mills (also advertising as 'wig makers'). At No 14 was Miles & Son, saddlers and tobacconists, run by J. & F. Mills. They advertised 'Rubber Boots repaired by special ROBI process' and stocked sports goods and hunting materials. Apart from their products, they are probably best remembered for the large dummy horse in one of their windows – I believe it was auctioned when the shop closed. There followed, at No 15, W. Bragg, sports and travel good depot. They were also agents for Meccano, Hornby and Dublo trains. Owned by 'Billy' Bragg, an ardent cricket fan, this building has very fond memories for me as I spent many pleasant hours in the front room above the shop playing billiards, snooker and table tennis with his son Colin (who later ran the shop), 'Flash' Hodge and Leslie Groombridge. I wonder what happened to the last two?

At Nos 16 & 17, one of the few High West Street buildings remaining as it was in 1939, was the old Ship Inn with publican Rene R. Pearson. It was followed at No 18 by the Spinning Wheel Restaurant, run by J.W. & E.S. Cuff. Another well-known grocers was next at No 19 – Fares Stores, with Rex Fare in charge. They offered 'motor deliveries to all parts'. At No 20 the Royal Oak Hotel, managed in 1939 by W. Mears. No 21 was a private residence, in 1939 occupied by R. Loveless, G.H. Moxom and A.J.B. Shephard while at No 22 was D.E. Jameson, Confectioner & Tobacconist. Next door at No 23 was the wholesale picture framemakers, Hills & Rowney, proprietor A. Edmondson and at No 33A, E. Feltham, stationer and newsagent.

At No 24 was the Britannic Assurance Co. Ltd with manager N.C. Smith, the Dorchester Commercial Typewriting and Shorthand School run by D.M. Meech and the Dorchester RDC Offices, Public Health and Rating Departments.

The Britannic Assurance is still there. The next building was the Catholic Church of Our Lady Queen of Martyrs, now a museum of Tutankhamun.

On the other side of Alington Street was, at No 27, Lee Motor Works (Bournemouth Ltd). In 1939 they were advertising 'Have you tried the new Vauxhall 12/4 Deluxe model for less than £200 and the 10 HP standard saloon at £168.00?' No 27 also housed Maison Chatele, ladies hairdressing salon, then managed by G.R. Cotter. How the memory plays tricks – I would have thought Frank Herring would have been there in 1939. A dental surgeon, W.G.H. North occupied No 28 with, next door at No 29, photographers W.H. Cumming (Mrs Webb). I was regularly taken there for 'growing-up' photographs. No 30 was Napper & Sons Motor & Cycle Engineers, run by Mrs S.A. Napper and Reg Inkpen. Reg was a well-known cricketer – a wicket keeper, I seem to remember, who at one time played for West Stafford in the Dorchester & District Evening League, as my father also did. J.P. Sandy, dairy and refreshments, were at No 31, and at 32 the Wessex Tea Rooms, then run by T.F. Rawnsley advertising 'home made cakes & preserves'. This was also the HQ of the Wessex Chess Club.

At No 33 Albert Edward Wiggins, Wireless dealer and the Misses M. & J. Trapp, handicrafts. At No 34 was the sub post office and stationer L. Lock. The only reminder today is a posting box in the wall. Worths' Fish Restaurant, managed by Charlie Worth, was at No 35, followed at No 36 by Legg, the confectioners run by Frank Wallbridge. They claimed 'Best English cooked meats a speciality'. In 1939 there was no number 37, and at No 38 was the Dorset Women's Institute (Miss Gladys M. Cole, county secretary). No number 39 is listed in 1939 and the last building in High West Street, at No 40, was occupied by Dr H.G. Harvey, Roy Salkeld (Saturdays by appointment) and C.W. Pike.

Although not a building, the final structure in High West Street is listed in 1939 as 'telephone call box'.

Across the road and next to Thomas Hardy's memorial statue at the Top O'Town in 1939 stood – at No 41 – the dentist's S.J. Stevens. I have cause to remember 'Sid', who once caused me much pain by removing a tooth with abcess attached . . . it's not a building with happy memories for me! He had three sons, Dennis, Alan and Edward and a daughter, Beryl, known to her colleagues in Lloyds Bank as 'Flossie'. Next door, at Savernake House (No 42), was C.W. Pike, Architect, followed by J.E.P. Winzar trading as J. Winzar & Son, House Decorators at No 43. At No 44 was the Old Tea House with, in 1939, Miss L.L. King as the proprietress. Happily, these delightful tea rooms are still going strong today and long may they continue to do so.

At No 45 and now long-gone, was Merchants Garage – distributor for Hillman and Sunbeam Talbot cars and then run by T.W. Merchant. In 1939 they were advertising: 'any make supplied and serviced. Cars for hire and fully equipped workshops'. They were also the official Tecalemit Station. The building also housed the Kleen-e-se Brush Co., the Dorset County Nursing Association and the Dorset Mental Welfare Association. 'Chance Cottage' at No 46 was Miss Kirbys' Guest House, while at No 47 was Napper & Son, Motor Engineers. Dr G. Osprey Taylor occupied No 48, followed at No 49 by T.B. Jeffs & Son, Auctioneers and Valuers, and the Halifax Building Society – dare I mention that locally they were fondly referred to as Mutt and Jeffs?

No 50 High West Street was the home for several departments of Dorset County Council Agricultural Committee, Director T.R. Ferris, Assistant Director F.E. Stanford, Officer for Agricultural Education Ralph Whiteman, Horticultural Lecturer T.P.P. MacPhail, Agricultural Lecturer W.E. Richards, Poultry Instructionesses Miss D.M. Evans and Miss M.A. Blore, and the Weights & Measures HQ – Chief Inspector, J. MacKinnon. At No 51 was the solicitors Thos Coombs & Morton and at No 5 A.J.R.R. Judson, Ladies' & Men's Tailors. Their advertisement stated: 'One of the oldest firms in one of the oldest premises with always the newest goods'. No 51 is now occupied by Jackson Stops and Staff.

No 52 was the hostel of Genge & Co and, at No 53, was solicitors Lock, Reed & Lock. This building is well known to me as my father worked there as a solicitor's clerk. I often fondly polish the silver salver presented to him which is inscribed 'FREDERICK CHURCHILL from H.O. LOCK in grateful appreciation 1898-1948' – 50 years of faithful service. The building looks almost the same today as I remember it in 1939 with the same steps and pillars leading to what I suspect, are the same front doors. You can also still see the archway at the end of the building, through which my father wheeled his bicycle. In 1939 Major H.O. Lock was the senior partner and it was he who wrote my reference for my clerkship at Lloyds Bank. Other members of staff were Joe Gillam, Norman Leslie and a Mr Morris. Also housed in the building was the Dorchester & District Register Office, the Clerk to Dorchester Rural District Council, the Superintendent Registrar; the Clerk to Dorchester Rural Rating Authority and the Clerk to South Dorset Assessment Committee.

Next door, at No 54, was Madame Rousse, Milliners – proprietor D.H. Overend, followed at No 55 by the Misses A. & E. Street, Costumiers & Ladies' Tailors. The ladies' and gentlemen's hairdressers, Stickland & Rendall, were at No 56. At No 57, was W. Snook, House Furnishers. Also occupying No 57 was the Dorset Territorial Army Association with its secretary, Lt. Col. J.V. Shute.

Glydepath Road (or Shire Hall Lane as it used to be known as) separated the next large building – Shire Hall, which was built in 1796/7 and contained the Assize Court. It is often incorrectly identified as the venue for the trials conducted by the infamous Judge Jeffreys, but it is where the 1834 trial of the Tolpuddle Martyrs, who were departed to Botany Bay, took place. In 1939 No 58 was listed as County House, whose caretaker was T.D. Davidge. No 59 then housed various Dorset County Council departments – Clerks, Air Raid Precautions, Surveyors, Accountants, Public Assistants and the Register of Birth & Deaths for Dorchester & District. Caretaker, E.W. Riggs. There are no numbers 60 or 61 listed for 1939, the next being No 62, Thorp Antiques, proprietor R.C. West. On the corner with Grey School Passage at No 63, Born Electrical Engineering Co with S.M. Oborn. The building is now occupied by an optician.

On the other side of Grey School Passage was the then Church of England Holy Trinity Church, where my father was leading chorister and the 'man of the cloth' was the Rev Joseph Pulliblank. Next, at No 64 were ironmongers, Thurman, managed by G.W. Watts. This was another store where one could buy just a few screws and nails. Their wares filled the pavement outside the shop, which is now a building society's office. The next building – Handle House – contained, at No 65, a confectioners run by Miss Angle and I still recall the mouthwatering chocolates they sold. At No 65A was Rogers' Music Saloon run by Mrs O. Rogers. This was the last shop in High West Street as the final two builidngs were at No 66 – Dorset County Museum with curator Lt. Col. C.D. Drew and attendant F. Hammett and opening hourse of 10am-1pm and 2pm-6pm, and then came the C of E church, St Peter's, also bordering on North Square. St Peter's Church holds special memories for me for it was there I was married to the late Charlotte (Beryl) Gillingham, the service being performed by the Rev. Alfred Wilkinson Markby (stipend in 1939, £374 per annum). When we appeared outside after the ceremony, Lloyds Bank opposite came to a virtual stop with all our bank colleagues waving from the doors and windows.

Trinity Street. The first building, although technically in Great Western Road was – in 1939 and still there today – The Junction Hotel. Then came Bowling Alley Walk and South Grove Cottage, occupied in 1939 by J.H. Maunder. This was followed by the Borough of Dorchester Electricity Department showrooms and offices. Next door was the Borough Fire Station – what memories! – who can possibly forget the two well-polished and gleaming fire engines and the thrill of hearing the alarm, seeing the red doors open and one, or both of them rushing out with clanging bell and crew struggling into their uniforms. It is very sad that the Fire Station is no longer there. In 1939, A.R. Jeffery was the captain.

Next came the Corporation Yard for Carriers Garage as it was described and then the County Library (Dorchester branch) – hours of attendance, weekdays (except Thursday) 2-4 and 6-8. Next door was Crabb & Co. Garages. In 1939 they were advertising that they had for sale 'the

Ford 'eight' at £115'. Happy days! Nos 17 to 20 were private houses while at No 21 was auctioneers Symonds & Sampson, manager A.T. Early. At No 22 was another private residence and at 22A-23 was Crabb & Co., 'Authorised Ford Dealers' (also the Excide Service Station, New Auto Factors). Another of Crabb's adverts proclaimed: 'We are the people to see'. At No 27 was Harry Gilday's Bluebird Cafe, while Nos 28 to 30 were more private houses and at No 30A was hairdressers Turner Bros – how often I climbed the stairs for the traditional 'short back and sides'. Next, at Nos 31 and 32, was, and still is, the Plaza Cinema and Café – J.A. Makinson, manager. Next door to The Plaza and at No 33 was A.H. Angell, Plumber and Decorator (Showrooms), also housing the Inland Revenue Office and Collector of Taxes. Angell's, whose office and works were in Princes Street, portrayed the Aga Registered Trademark on their advertisements.

Nos 34 to 36 were private houses, while at No 37 was The Girl Pat Fish Bar, proprietor H.G. Diament. The registered office of Dorchester Comrades Club Ltd, with steward W.R. Pufer was at No 38 – also the British Legion Office (Dorchester Branch) and next door at No 39, the Royal London Mutual Insurance Society Ltd with W.E. Udle as inspector. At No 40 was L.F. Beal, Electrician, with Genges taking over the remaining spaces before reaching the corner with High West Street.

Crossing over to the other side of Trinity Street was a long building, part of Godwins China shop whose registered number was in High West Street. Then came the rear entrance of the Antelope Hotel followed by T. Ensor & Sons' saleroom. At No 3 was Dental Surgeon C.F. Long – not many happy memories for me in view of the number of visits paid there. Still, as the result of one visit, I managed to get a date with the very attractive receptionist, Joyce (I will spare her blushes by omitting her surname). The next building was the *Dorset County Chronicle* and *Southern Times* Newspapers Ltd Office and Printing Works. Then came Boons stores garage, followed by Cedar Park Villas. There followed the rear entrances to Marks & Spencers and Woolworths, then Frys Home-Made Bread and Tilleys Motor Garage. Before

New Street was the rear entrance of Buglers and the Post Office.

On the other side of New Street was H. Nesham, boot repair workshops, R.J. Watts' Used Car Depot and the rear entrance of Matthews, Wilfrid Snook, Radio and Furniture, and Frys Dairy. After the passage to South Street was, and still is, the George Hotel licensee in 1939, Mrs A.M. Laming. At No 12 was the London & Scottish Assurance Corporation Ltd, resident inspector L.E. May, and at No 13 G. Bryer Ash, Coal Merchants, – this was their receiving office. At the end of Trinity Street, at No 14, was Tilleys Motor Cycle Repair Works.

Much of Trinity Street has been rebuilt since 1939. Between the present Iceland Store and Parys Dry Cleaning, only two original buildings remain. Further along, on the same side, it is all new from the Plaza Cinema to the Trinity Club. On the other side, most of the buildings between the Horse with the Red Umbrella to the Tourist Office are also new. As is the large building between the rear of Woolworths and the GPO – it has a tablet inscribed '1988'. Although there are many photographs of the other main streets in Dorchester to be found, Trinity Street appears to have been neglected.

North Square (off Cornhill). From Cornhill, the first building both in 1939 and now, although with its entrance in High West Street, was St Peter's Church. In 1939 at No 1 North Square was Voss Bros, Butchers (Alfred Charles Voss T/A), followed at No 2 by the Soldiers Home Refreshment Rooms with Miss Taylor in charge. These Georgian buildings were demolished in the 1960s to house the recently closed Kwik Fit. At No 3 was W. Jewell, Plumber (also the secretary of Progress AOF) and at No 4 was R.H. Jewell, Watchmaker and Jeweller. The last building before Colliton Street was No 5, which housed the 'Fried Fish Shop' of E.J. Wood.

On the other side of Colliton Street – at No 6 and now a restaurant – was W.A. Hull, General Engineer (I remember it more as a Plumbers store). Next was, and still is, H.M. Prison. In 1939 Major R.O. Bridgeman was Governor and Mr Stavey, Chief Prison Officer. Then came Nos 1 to 11 Castle Row, which housed prison officers, followed by Friary Hill and Frome Terrace and the

Liberal Hall.

After Orchard Street, at No 8, North Square, was Chubbs Almshouses, still today proudly proclaiming the name on the side of the building. No 9 was a private house and in No 10 was T.Burt & Son, Coal Merchants. Nos 11 to 14 were also private residences with, at No 15, the Half Moon, H. Moore as licensee. No 16 housed W. Sturmey, Hairdresser. No 17 was a private house, followed at No 18 by J.C. Brown, Grocer – Cecil kept a small but well-stocked shop but in 1939 as a dog lover, I was far more interested in his Alsatian dog, than in what he sold. No 19 was a private house with, at No 20, The Dorchester Arms with its landlord of the time, H. Harris. No 21 housed the Municipal Offices with the offices of the Town Clerk, Borough Survey, Water Engineer and Sanitory Inspector. Joseph Rippen was the Hall Keeper and Sergeant-at-Mace. The 1939 records lists Market House with R. Bubier, Butcher, A.C. Voss, Butcher and W.H. Christopher, Butcher as the occupants. The building still has on the wall 'Police Station and Market'. At the side of the Corn Exchange I seem to remember, there was a gentleman's lavatory. There are very few photographs of North Square in the county archives.

Great Western Road. I am delighted to see today one shop that was there in 1939 – White & Sons, Boot Makers. Mr White was a polite and helpful man and I bought all my shoes there. I went to my first school with his son George just across the road from his shop – Miss Kensett's Kindergarten, with teachers Miss Kensett herself and Miss Lewis.

Other shops I remember – but are sadly now all gone – were, at No 40, F.R. Herring, Picture Frame Makers (but at least still elsewhere in Dorchester), C.L. Parsons, Hairdresser and Tobacconist, at No 35, with a large advertisement painted on its walls – The Weymouth and District Co-operative Society at No 32, which as a large store with wide steps leading to the door way (and receiving your 'divvy stamps' with each purchase), and butchers A.G. Holland at No 22.

At the top of the street was the Great Western Hotel – a typical railway hotel – and across from the GWR station approach, the large premises of Webb, Major and Co., Timber Merchants.

Alongside was the cafe run by Miss Ash, G. Bryer Ash Ltd, Coal Office, and the Dorset Farmers Ltd store.

Icen Way. The building I most remember in Icen Way was the old YMCA now converted into housing. I was a Youth Leader in my early days, this was when the Rev. Thomas was in charge and Mr Birch was secretary; he also being a probation officer, we often had as 'guests' several of the boys under his care. In those days the YMCA had a very good cricket XI which played in the Dorchester & District Evening League (I remember Fred Alderman as a fast bowler, Bert Hayes, Louis Dobell, wicket keeper Ken Cornick, Arthur Hinton and many more). We also had a good football XI (Jimmy Clare as centre half, Jimmy Lawler in goal, Laurie Bowen and Ray Stevens are names that come to mind), as well as teams in the snooker and billiards leagues. There was also a championship-winning team that several times topped the Dorchester & District Table Tennis League. I was captain, other players being John Feltham, John Dowden and Gordon Sturmey all, sadly no longer with us.

Opposite the YMCA was a blacksmiths – William Stickland – 'A trial order respectfully solicited'. Bill, or 'Jingle' as he was known to his friends, could wield a cricket bat with the same dexterity as he wielded his heavy horse-shoeing tools. It's another old business sadly gone. Perhaps the one place in Icen Way that has not been missed, especially the smell, is the Gas Works. It is strange how the memory plays tricks as I felt sure there were two large green gasometers on site, but I have been assured there were, and have seen, the remains of three.

I have covered the main shopping/business areas of Dorchester in 1939 but, of course, there were many other well known buildings and businesses long since gone:

That wonderful ironmongers in Prince's Street – E.W. Venton – another store that stocked everything and where you could purchase small quantities. Their 1939 'advert' stated 'The right goods at the right price (consistent with quality), combined with courtesy and service'. I well remember both the shop and playing table tennis against one of the sons, Terry who played for 'The Lofters' in those days. Also in Princes Street, at No 3, I remember the Plume of Feathers public house.

Then there was the Dorchester Steam Laundry in Bridport Road 'Established over 60 years', Lott and Walne, the foundry who offered 'Prompt and efficient service', T.F. Adams in London Road 'Horses removed by up-to-date Horse Boxes'.

Robert Lush in The Grove who, in 1939, advertised 'Undertaker – also General Repairs'. The mind boggles!

As a young boy, I was fascinated by the gleaming steam rollers and traction engines in the yard of Eddison Steam Rolling Company Ltd in Allington Road. And it seemed that wherever one was in Dorchester at 12.30 p.m, the loud siren emitting from their premises at that time, could be heard.

Then there was the Victoria Park Creamery in Alice Road who stated in 1939, 'We have pleasure in informing our many customers that we now sell Tuberculin Tested Guernsey and Shorthorn milk from Accredited Farms'. They were then the sole agents for Bladen Dairies Ltd, A.L. Scott was Manager.

Meyers, timber and general builders merchants in Damers Road, yet another business to have gone. As has, another builder, Charles E. Slade in Acland Road.

Even the Dorset County Hospital in Princes Street is no longer a hospital, although thankfully most of the main buildings remain and are being converted into town houses.

Thankfully, the Borough Gardens, complete with clock and fountain remain: R.J. Trim was head gardener in 1939. For most of us without cars, this was our main 'courting' area. I well remember watching some thrilling tennis 'doubles' matches played on the public courts involving Fred Alderman, George Grundy, Jack Rogers and Kubo.

Also remaining is the market in Weymouth Avenue although I do miss the pens of sheep and pigs and the hustle and bustle of the animals being loaded and unloaded from the many assorted lorries. In 1939 the majority of people attending were from the farming community, as against today's bus loads of people coming from all over the county for clothes, shoes, plants etc. etc.. Almost opposite the market and still there, the Police Station. In 1939 Major Lionel Peel Yates was the Chief Constable.

The Eldridge Pope Brewery building is of course still here but how I miss those wonderful, well-groomed, horses pulling a dray piled with beer casks (made of wood in 1939). I can still see the horses eating from their nose-bags when they were at rest.

Both railway stations are still here, although British Rail today instead of the Great Western Railway and Southern Railway as they were in 1939. Having been born in a house overlooking the Southern Railway, I fondly remember the days of steam. In those days trains from Weymouth to Waterloo needed to come up past Culliford Road bridge before they could reverse back into the station. Opposite where I lived at 144 Monmouth Road was both the coal loading and unloading bays and on the Prince of Wales Road side a large loading bay which Bertram Mills Circus would use. What excitement to see the lions, tigers, giraffes etc. when the 'Circus came to town'. Often the elephants would walk to their usual venue in Weymouth Avenue. Their circus was in Dorchester in 1939.

Obviously having been born in Monmouth Road, that road and the immediate surrounding area hold many memories. Two doors above our house was Bishops Bakery – 'For the best bread in Town'. 'Bert' ran the shop with his wife, daughters Marie and Bertha, and son Cecil. This was the typical corner shop of its time – selling most items – their buns were known throughout the county and much sought after by the boys from the Grammar School some 100 yards away. These were the days of ½d chews, sherbert dips, liquorice sticks, 'gobstoppers' and packets of lemonade crystals. Oh the memories! Being a dog lover I remember their old dog 'Jim', who I was allowed to walk 'provided I did not go too far' – whether this was for the dog's benefit or mine, I never did find out! In Bishop's yard was a garage in which the loft was used for table tennis. (The team name 'Lofters' comes as no surprise). My cousin Betty Sadler was a member of this team.

Acknowledgments

I am extremely grateful to all my many friends, acquaintances and former strangers who freely gave their time. There are far too many list them all, but an especial thank you is owed to the Curator of the Dorset County Museum, Mr Ted Brewer, Miss Valerie Dicker, the late Mr John Hedger, Mr Ray Lake, Miss Claire Pinder, Mr Brian Toop and Mr David Whitefield.

I am grateful to the following for allowing the inclusion of illustrations in their possession or for which they hold the copyright:

Simon Adamson, page 21 (top); Terry Bishop, 65; Nigel J. Clarke Publications, 68; Dorset County Museum, 11, 13, 14, 20, 27, 29, 38, 46, 52, 55, 63, 65 (top), 66, 73, 74, 76, 90, 91, 93, 96, 97, 105; Jim Foot, 59, 61; Tony Hewitt, 26; Imperial War Museum, 58; Miss Evelyn Kingman, 103; the Parsons family, 94, 95, 100; Mrs Marcella Perham, 78, 79; Miss Winzar, 25.

The remaining illustrations come from the collections of the author and the Dovecote Press.

I am grateful to Christopher Chaplin for drawing the maps on pages 6, 7, 8, 9, 10 and the maps showing bomb damage on pages 70 and 71.